HER

I'M STILL STANDING

The Chronicles Of 11 Amazing Women

Melissa Williams

Forward By
Dr. Jamal H. Bryant
Melody S. Holt

Forward By
Dr. Jamal H. Bryant

When Jesus chose the 12 disciples, he was metaphorically representing the 12 tribes of Israel. What my friend and sister has cultivated in this compelling anthology "HER" penetrates the human experience in sharp alto and soprano voices. These sisters aren't survivors but overcomers! Dr. King coined the expression "the priesthood of all believers," suggesting that everyone with a testimony has a ministry. The chronicles of these superheroes story stir up faith and revitalize hope that the impossible is indeed possible. This book, which is about women is not just for women but for anybody birthed by "HER."

History is always slanted to the advantage of those who write it. Hence the great exploits of time performed by women have mostly been muted. With the significant role women have played in history it's borderline unfathomable that of the 66 books in the Bible only one is named after a woman. Jesus forewarned that some of the greatest miracles would transpire after he left the earth. Those who were skeptical will be converted and challenged to believe. Every woman's testimony underscores the possibility for us to become more than a conqueror. What started as a drama ends as a thriller.

The late dr Myles Monroe before his demise lamented, " the best ideas are found in the cemetery because people die with what they should have lived with. Melissa Williams has dared to live her truth out loud and operates as a magnet to pull 10 others in. Now imagine how 1000 more will catch on fire because of the fuse ignited on these pages. As a pastor, author and philanthropist I see evangelism , encouragement and coaching coming into praxis. The impact will reach beyond a best seller but navigate to a self help blue print. The instance is shared in the gospel for the one delivered to identify who was the conduit.... after people are set free by the millions and the investigation is launched as to who ushered in the breakthrough the four corners of the earth will resoundingly echo ....HER

Forward By
Melody S. Holt

Since the beginning of time, women have been portrayed as the lesser, weaker sex. But from the beginning of time, we've been fighters. Women have fought for the right to work, to vote, for equal pay, for control of their minds and bodies, and we continue to fight against generational traumas.

To suggest that women are lesser or weaker could not be further from the truth.

Instead, women are resilient and HER is a vivid example of our ability to rebound.

As a wife and mother of four, I know all too well that no matter how much you plan for the life of your dreams that plan can be unexpectedly derailed. In the midst of it all, you feel like you're alone. You literally have no clue that other women have experienced the same. For some reason, we've been conditioned to suffer in silence. We've been taught to quietly wear our pain as a badge of honor. And while we are putting on strong faces for those around us, we are slowly dying on the inside.

That's why stories like those told in HER are so important. More women need to know and understand that they are not alone. The scars, pain, and hurt are not unique. There are women who understand and can offer guidance. There are women who can help us hold it together until we are ready to move forward in whichever way we choose.

The author of HER, Melissa Williams, truly has a heart for facilitating healing among women through shared stories and ideas. Likewise, the women who have decided to share their stories in the pages of Melissa's book are bold.

They are survivors. They are resilient.

Just like you.

Take each of the stories that you will read as a testament to the fact that you are never, ever alone. There are others who have gone before you. They've made it out of their pain and are on to a new level. Now, it's your turn.

CONTENTS

INTRODUCTION

"When she speaks, her words are wise, and she gives instructions with kindness. "- Proverbs 31:26(NLT)

Sometimes, the story of a million voices can be heard through the unrehearsed and piercing sound waves we call words that come from the core of a woman's soul. It has many sounds and many shades. Her many sounds represent the defining and distinguishing shades of life's visible and unseen triumphs and tragedies. Metaphorically speaking, it can be compared to the multi colors of a rainbow after a storm that affirms peace is on the rise, and very soon, the sun will rise again. When she laughs, those around her feel the joy that exudes from her giggle. It is the sound of blissful excitement on her wedding day that somehow becomes the rhythm of joyful expressions, and the heartbeat of love in the room as she embraces the journey of covenant and commitment.

It is the welcoming sound of celebration when she has given birth to a child, and yet when tears roll down her face, she often does not have a sound, but the heaviness of her presence has a shattering effect that informs those around her that trouble or sadness is present. She has a sound that resonates with those that can identify with what is frequently unspoken but seen.

Very often, we find that a woman sees more than she says and gives more than she receives. She may often live a life in some truths never to be shared, spoken, or revealed. Some pains will never fully heal, and some dreams never to be lived.

A woman, not all women, but many of her kind, decide daily to make a conscious chess move, not because she does not know the truth, or feel its breath blowing over her shoulders, but for the lives she serves, loves, protects, guides, cherish, and honors. She may often put herself last so that the people in her life can be first. She will walk through the fire, so the ones she loves will never feel the flames or the heat of life. She will go without eating, so her child will never know what it feels like to be hungry. She, the woman knows her strengths but seldom reveals her weakness because she knows that she is someone's SHERO.

A woman often chooses to live a life in the shadow of the unspoken....

She is HER...

"Strong Black woman " the Unspoken Profanity

We are called strong black women, with melanin skin and with a hint of Caramel for sweetness. We are the epitome of beauty and brilliance in many shades and sizes, but yet with distinguishing skin tones that make us uniquely captivating and charming and also breathtaking to some. The conceptual ideology of a strong black woman identifies women of color as victims of intersectionality within a patriarchal society in which they are forced to fit the standard mold of a traditional strong black woman versus what it means to be a woman to themselves.

It's in HER eyes that will reveal the soul of who we are, where we come from, and the history of our ancestors, but yet the awakening of a new movement that is rarely discussed. Used interchangeably, the "Black Superwomen Myth " is the pressure and expectation of a woman of color to balance numerous roles of the mother, worker, homemaker, student, and any other roles that are usually inclusive to one person or sex. Allow me to remind you; this is different from a career woman because rather than sacrifice the role that supports her family in order to excel in her career, the superwoman, or as titled in the new wave. " BOSS CHIC" is forced to support both the traditional Suzy homemaker role and a career woman. However, there is an undeniable worldwide movement that has evolved into a silent interference to be witnessed by racial onlookers that can attest to the lives of millions of black queens around the world. The four runners of our time are Black African American women who are leading ladies that have unapologetically become global voices as leaders, teachers, activists, and healers who are doing powerful, transformative work in the world. It appears for the legacy and history of slavery and the fight for women's rights, equal justice, and just for women to be treated with respect, for our beloved ancestors, we as women are making a mark in the earth that boldly reveals that the injustice they suffered will not be in vain.

"A Strong Black "HER" ...

It's in the eyes of every black woman, the mother, daughter, sister, cousin, niece, the lawyer, full-time mom, the political analyst, the women's rights leader, and the millions of us who are without a title, still does not define us. It's in the eyes of the African American woman who has not identified herself as the world would like to label her as black, ugly and dumb. Some people have belittled her character, and yet every morning, she awakens to give an imperfect world her presence and substance to be a change agent in society. Here lies the truth of the strong black women's story that may never be told because, in a world that has marginalized her existence, it has also become her fortitude for millions, and for others it has become their embrace and motivation. This mold of being self-reliant and self-contained is damaging in a sense because if you are unable to be self-sufficient and/or self-contained then culturally you aren't a true strong black woman, and you aren't to be depended upon. The truth is, we have been taught by our cultural and unspoken expectations which is to us a comparison to biblical law. Internally within the hearts of many women we are to be the backbone of our families. We are taught that we should be strong and resilient. But what happens when the strong become weak?

She carries invisible luggage from day to day, from place to place and often, it brings "HER" to a standstill. She bends, only to gain enough strength to Stand, she will catch HER breath, but never break.

4

"HER"... Bend But Don't Break

I remember when my father, at the young age of 59 unexpectedly had a massive heart attack, the day before the heart attack my dad decided to surprise me, and he came to my office at the outreach center for me to finalize a letter for the judge for one of the men in a shelter he had asked me to permit to volunteer as his community service. My dad is a philanthropist. His passion and heart were always seen in the way he served others. He never met a stranger, and to know him is to know that beautiful smile that can light up a room. My dad and I sat in my office for almost 4 hours, just talking and laughing!!. He was consigning with me to run for the Political office of Mayor in the city I resided in at the time. But within the conversation he would repeatedly say how tired he was and he could not wait for him and my mom to take their dream vacation in a few weeks. He was so excited to take this vacation that he was talking about. He could finally take my mom on a real vacation that she would love. (*that's what my mom calls it. "Real."*) You see, my dad, well let's just say was a workaholic, so he never took days off or time away from Pastoring or his corporate job. So this week's vacation was going to be used very wisely. Well, he said a honeymoon. Seeing that, my dad and mom had just renewed their vows eight months earlier. But here again, he sat back in the office chair in front of my desk and took a deep breath, and as I looked into his eyes and face as he stated again " I'm tired." He was so seemingly tired, and I told him to go home to rest. That same night my dad suffered a massive heart attack and sadly passed away three days later. Because I have always been the strong daughter and woman, the night he passed at the hospital, I had no one to ask me, " if I was ok." The conversation was, "Melissa, what are you going to do about the arrangements"? And the love for my mother outweighed my broken heart. So from that night I left My father to rest in Peace at the hospital, I, in turn, took my mother home to live with me. The moment my father passed away, I suddenly became the person responsible for every decision and everyone. Instantly, the night he passed I became the backbone of my immediate family, I never stopped to grieve, and I never took a moment to self medicate my hurt, lost or thought about my father not being with me anymore. My focus was on my mother and two brothers; It was on the family and trying to keep a clear head, I had to intentionally position my pain-filled heart and grief behind making arrangements for his burial while also being the voice Of comfort to his wife of over thirty years. I had to decide what funeral home would come to transport his body from the hospital. I had to contact my family, the insurance company, the funeral home. I was the strength to some and the voice of comfort for many. From picking out the casket to helping my mom select the suit he will be buried in. Choosing his last suit and tie that he would wear down to his socks. It was a lot mentally and emotionally but yet, being the strong black woman and now silently suppressed grieving daughter, I couldn't miss a beat.

Do not grieve, for the joy of the Lord is your strength.
Nehemiah 8:10

There are so many women who feel guilty because they think if they don't continue to live in the visage or this expectation of the "Strong woman" that they will lose the respect of some peers and family.

When a woman has no choice but to be strong all the time without a chance to breathe, anything that isn't related to fulfilling all the roles that are needed is suppressed, such things as sadness or pain, because its deemed weakness. This silent expectation of social paradoxes can create a suicidal environment, and self-contradiction, which is not enough, and that is damned if it does, damned if you don't; this is stigma for black women across the diaspora. Historically, due to her strength and love, this stigma is what held black families together because of the systemic lack of strong balanced male authority is the same thing that is killing our women today.

However, our intelligent minds have, for years, been underestimated. We've always created or discovered a resolution to pave a new path that was never designed for us. But it has aligned our internal awareness to walk down a path that gives direction to self-awareness, self-love, self-development, and self-confidence. We are to rise above the stigma that society has labeled many black women and as we possess our history and give life to a brighter future, we are Sculpting a class all by ourselves. The beauty we exemplify is more than skin deep. However, The cognitive

7

disagreement between the "real woman" versus the "ideal woman" consequently causes strain on a woman's interpersonal relationship with significant others, extended families, and their immediate community as a whole. It's more than The Idea of being HER….

The voices of a thousand people cannot compare to the voice of one strong woman. For when she speaks HER truth, she sounds the alarm for the masses and gives freedom to others once held captive by silence.

CHAPTER 1

MELISSA WILLIAMS

HER TRUTH

Her parents got divorced when she was three, and she and her brother went to live with their grandmother in Stamps, Arkansas. When she was eight, she was raped by her mother's boyfriend. When she revealed what happened, her uncles kicked the culprit to death. Frightened by the power of her tongue, this young lady made a choice not to speak for the next five years.

A poet and novelist. Born in St. Louis, Missouri. Maya Angelou-born Marguerite Johnson is HER....

She is frightened by HER words that revealed HER truth that she silently feels caused death. Afraid that not only is the power in her words detrimental, but it is now a weapon revealed and proven to be an available force she has that can be constructive, bring healing, hurt, or harm but has dunamis power to provoke effective change. She understands speaking words of truth has an energy that is volatile. HER words have the ability to bring despair, conviction, and pain. So maybe if she doesn't speak, her words will only remain constant thoughts. Could it be possible that silence will sustain life? I'm not sure which one erupts changes in the lives of individuals, but her thought caused such an amazing gift as her words to be silent, but I now realize the silence of one's truth can also be the pathway to finding strength in a voice that was once afraid.

You can find your voice when you embrace your inner strength. You can awaken your soul when you allow the pain in your life to become the secret introduction to your purpose to live and to pursue your passion. I know what death feels like from speaking words that I saw manifest. I, too know the weight of carrying a silent pain, but then I realized pain never shows up alone. It will always come alongside its companion: FEAR.

THE REFLECTIONS OF FEAR

False Evidence Appearing Real

When I am afraid, I will put my trust in you. Psalm. 56:3

Fear is the robbery of hope. It is designed to keep you safe, but not soaring. Fear is the detour on the road to success and the roadmap to stagnation. Fear's ultimate goal is to rob you of your future while keeping you focused and afraid of the "what ifs" and the "whys." What if I lose my house? What if I get sick? What if they don't love me? What if my past gets revealed? What if I fail? What if my marriage ends? The What ifs are not the voice of reasoning but the screams of an internal awakening, that fights against your potential to BE. It is like a person on life support that cannot breathe on his or her own, but people are talking to you and waiting for a response. It slowly robs you of life. Fear has the hope of your heart in limbo with the WHYs.

Why did that happen to me? Why did my father abandon me? Why did he/she molest me? Why did I have an abortion? Why did I make that choice? Why did my life have to be so hard? Why me? The " what ifs" and the "whys" are the reflections of Fear because it always leads to the unanswered questions that only faith and hope have the answers to.

Simply put, because faith is the substance of things hoped for and the evidence of things not seen, we sometimes judge prematurely by our natural eyes, the situations, and the people. Do you understand now? So why is fear always hanging around your life? Fear's ultimate goal is the weapon used to blind you of your sight from vision to see your future or your next. The tactic is to misrepresent that your future is much brighter than today's fear, while slowly robbing your passion for believing for tomorrow will cause you to realize that within you is everything you need to do more and become greater. So, many people fail to acknowledge that fear is one of the most patient emotions.

An emotion is a natural instinctive state of mind derived from one's circumstances, instinctive or intuitive feeling as distinguished from reasoning or knowledge. Emotions can be defined as a positive or negative experience that is associated with a particular pattern of physiological activity. Emotions are complex. According

3

to some theories, they are states of feeling that result in physical and psychological changes that influence our behavior, just like compassion or happiness, anger, or excitement. But for some reason, we build the emotion of fear as the emotion that defines the art of our behavior to excel or prevail. We give it the most power to arrest our momentum for thriving, and it forces us to stop living out loud.

This emotion called FEAR, which stands for False Evidence Appearing Real gradually torments your thoughts that eventually stop the birthing of your creativity within. It attempts to impregnate your mind with negative scenarios, to abort the destiny your life has been predestined to live. Its subtle deceit is to distract you from the promise that you believe God has spoken concerning your life. It is designed to mentally weigh you down with the fear that it won't happen for you, as if you don't deserve good things to happen in your life or you don't deserve love. It makes you feel like your life will always remain the same, that maybe you don't deserve what you believe that God has for you will manifest in your life. Fear in areas of life can paralyze you into inaction. It will always be a dedicated and committed emotion to the relationship between the two of you. It will never want a divorce, and it will always run back to you as if it was never meant to hurt you. Fear, if given power by your own words, actions, and thinking will keep you stagnated. Its strength is only stronger when you both agree to remain as one. It somehow tries to control the key to your heart, mind, and soul if you don't change the lock. It never wants to give back ownership or say goodbye to a residence that it has lived in for years. The Bible says in:

2Timothy 1:7, "For God hath not given us the spirit of fear, but of power, and of love, and of a sound mind."

One minute, you evict the false evidence appearing real, but as soon as life starts to happen, we tend to welcome them back. We know God did not give it to us, but the text never said it wouldn't show up. But what do you do when it shows up? When it steals your peace of a sound mind? When its drive is to take over your power and ability to love? What then? If we are honest with no one but ourselves, we have all had an ongoing relationship with this emotion, time, and time again. Have you ever walked into a room, and behind you comes someone that pops out of nowhere that you were not expecting, and they scare you? You grab your heart instantly because of the sudden fear; you stop breathing and cease from whatever task you were performing for a few seconds. But once you see it's someone you know, you release your chest and say, " OMG! You scared me." Then momentarily you start to breathe again. It's a breath of relief.

Do you remember a similar incident? Can you remember how you felt? At that moment, you will realize that you were not in control as to what was happening in your life. Many times, we are not in control of the pop-ups in our life, and if we are not careful, these interruptions will prolong and delay us from our next season. It takes the rhythm of your life as if the balance of your life had just been shaken. It gripped your soul all at once. It shocked your core

5

because of the fear of who and what was about to happen. But after the initial shock and you resume to what you were previously doing, but in the corridor of your mind, you're still saying to yourself, "Ima get them."

I remember when my daughter was seven years old, and she traveled with me for an engagement I had to speak. She wanted to go swimming at the hotel with her friend that I had permitted to come with us. She was so excited because her little friend was with us and they loved the water. Well, her friend was nine and had taken swimming lessons before, so, her friend knew that it was going to be fun and a piece of cake. While on the other hand, my precious little seven years old just loved water and always wanted to be in it. The only issue was she hated the water when it came down to drinking it. Lol, So as time passed by, they were getting more and more excited. As we went to the pool area, I noticed the pool had a post on the wall as to how many feet each level was. Well, I said to my daughter, I know you are excited, but you can't go too far because it's too deep for you.

I noticed as she looked into the pool, her eyes were as a shining new penny. You could see the excitement, the urgency to swim, and the passion for just having fun. She looked at the pool with joy and had a huge smile on her face. Splash! Her little nine years old best friend jumps into the pool, and all I could hear is the splash of water as she leaped in. She's having the time of her life. Her best friend jumped in and yells with a loud, boisterous sound of laughter. As I turned to look at my sweet baby girl, I noticed the glare in her eyes started to turn dim, but she had this little semi smirk on her face. I Said to her, "Are you ready?"

She says, "um yes, I am ready."

She slowly walked towards the pool, and out of nowhere, I heard this light shaky voice say to me, "Mommie, How deep is the water?"

I look down only to witness the face of a child who's excitement is being interrupted by an emotion she has never felt. I began to explain to her the levels of the pool and why she must stay close to what she's comfortable in. Sometimes, it's not the fear of taking the risk that frightens us, it's the current of the tide or the waves of life that can be so unpredictable that makes us second guess, "is now the time?" or question ourself, "can I do this?" The risk in our life is the fear of drowning in a place we've never been trained in. Often, it's not the initial decision, but because ordinary and familiar is a comfort to us, we remain where we are, but we want different results. You can never have different results if you never go into deep water you've never attempted to swim in. You have to be willing to become someone you've never been before. I began to tell my daughter that the water is not what she is afraid of, knowing that you have never been into the deep where you can't control your movement.

I ask her again, "are you ready?'

"Yes." She says.

As she walked closer, I noticed she did not jump into the pool as her friend suggested, but she holds onto the rail that leads down the stairs into the pool. She slowly takes her time and walks down the steps one by one. As she recognizes this is unfamiliar, and I'm not sure if I'm ready or prepared enough to get into what's deeper than what I'm used to. She Walks in, the water comes to her feet, she takes a few more steps, the water comes to her knees, and the farther she goes, the water comes to her thigh. My brave daughter suddenly goes deeper, and the water reaches her waist. She suddenly stops, and her little friend says, "come over here with me." My little poo-poo looks at her Best friend and then looks at me with those big brown eyes and said, " Mommie, it's too deep over there, I'm going to stay right here where my feet can touch the ground."

Sometimes our greatest fear is not what we have already experienced, but the possibility of what could happen.

CONFRONTING THE HIDDEN

One thing I have to admit is that feelings are real, but it doesn't mean it's true. You can let fear drown you or drive you. I remember the morning I walked into my parents' room to tell them the hidden secret I had carried for years. I was no longer afraid of the pain or shame of being raped at an early age because I had lived my life carrying the shame of it in secret. I was scared of how my parents would feel. How my dad would look at me knowing his only daughter has withheld the reasons as to why her behavior and attitude has changed in the last few years. From being outgoing to

8

now withdrawn and angry, from being the daughter who was simply joyful, and her only dream was to sing, to being full of rage as a teen. My mom not knowing that for years, I was afraid of them being hurt by the truth that was hurting me. I feared because my parents, who were pastors in a religious denomination that preached hell and sanctification would judge me, a 14-year-old teen, or blame me. I did not know any better at that time due to the condemnation I had already experienced from them just for wearing lip gloss and nail polish. So, how would the church now look at me? Would my family believe me? I experienced all sorts of thoughts.

Fear will cause you to believe that the story or the lie in your mind will actually come true.

WHEN TIME MET DESTINY

To live your life based on a thought that may never come to past will camouflage the possibility of what can be...

I can recall the day the love of my life came into my life. He turned a girl's world upside down and inside out. His uncommon ability to be strong and sensitive. His willingness to believe that second chances are possible. From his mature grace and charm to the words of encouragement, support, peace, and comfort he brought into my life. He came into my life when love or the possibilities of a relationship was not a decision or desire to me. In other words, I was content with being single.

9

However, this six-foot gentle giant, intelligent, good looking, and Lord knows smelled divine, would speak to the part of my soul that no other person could even reach or dare to touch. His confidence in who he was as a man, father, leader, and friend allowed him to embrace a strong yet sensitive flawed woman that not many could see her insecurities. He spoke life to the part of the woman in me that was permitted to be the shy little girl at times, very silly and full of laughs, and yet the woman in me that only wanted to be his everything that he needed in a partner, friend, and lady. I wanted him to see the relentless sensitive woman, the caring mother, the CEO, and minister, but experience the love from a pure heart that was afraid to take a risk at love once more but was willing because it was him.

He filled my heart with so much happiness, possibilities, and words of adoration. His presence made me feel safe. He was the one that reached the part of my inner being that gave me permission to cry and be honest without feeling ashamed. He spoke to the very tough skin of me that had to be tough all my life. I secretly longed for the day it would be ok to be soft and vulnerable while not feeling obligated to take care of everyone but myself. He permitted me to take my cape off.

This gentle giant became my Superman, my ability to love freely, my joy when tough times hit. He became my sounding board when I had a new revelation, business idea, or concern for my children, and yet he was my fun time when I could just let my hair down and be his lady, not the Evangelist or the Woman of God. He was my balance. He let me be myself. Even though he honored the woman of God I am, I honored him even more. He gave me tough love at times that opened my eyes to see the flaws that I hadn't realized about me, and he said what others wouldn't say to me, but yet being a wise man, he handled me with grace and care when he knew what he had to say to me was going to be a hard pill to swallow.

God will use who you trust your heart with and situations that mean the most to you, to sometimes break you so you can become who he has predestined you to be.

What I didn't even realize was my bossy mannerisms and temperament. I had not realized the woman I had become due to life lessons and experiences had trained me to be a leader, a fighter, and a person who has always had to protect and defend herself. A lady who felt the need to take care of herself. Who at this point in her life didn't even know how to ask for help because, in times past, it was always me having to be there for me. I was the one who took care of others, so it was hard seeing myself silently defending who I was, but realized I wanted to be better. I had finally accepted the part of me that revealed I needed more self-development.

Always give yourself permission to grow and become a better you.

When you've had to be the fighter for so long, for so many reasons, it's hard to accept the day you're not in a boxing ring but, sitting at the dinner table, holding the hands of new life and

11

looking into the eyes of unconditional love. His welcoming and loving correction open the eyes of my heart to become a better me in so many ways. The woman who had on numerous times looked in the mirror but not seen her reflection was now ready and willing to see her true reflection and face the years of scars buried deep into the role of "I've had to be her all my life." It wasn't about the woman I had to be anymore, but the person, the woman, the mother, the friend, the lover whom I now wanted to be just COMPLETE.

The Beauty of it all is, it took time for me to see me because I have been this person for so long, I couldn't see where I needed to change previously. He celebrated me even in private when there was no one watching, and in a room of onlookers, I felt as if I was his dream girl especially when he called me His Angel. It's amazing how different seasons of your life will change your circle of relationships and awaken what has been sleeping in you while unlocking the areas of your life that you thought you had sealed and thrown away the key. I now realize that when God wants to mature and elevate you, he causes disconnections and discomfort.

This man captured my heart and made all my walls crumble into dust without a fight. It was almost unreal. He showed me through his words and actions that he was willing to love all of me. He was my best friend and more. He made me feel I could love again after years of feeling I'd never want to give my heart to anyone else. After becoming a successful person as a single mom in business and ministry, I was living a life of years of secret, shame, hurt, rejection, physical and emotional abuse, regrets, and silent embarrassment and all the pain of ever having loved. I now had finally met someone that could carry who I was and destined to become.

BREAKING THE SILENCE

Silence is the enemy of intimacy, yet silence is a source of strength.

I can remember the day I had to have a conversation with Destiny, who was the love of my life because I was having a hard time remembering. I was preparing for a test, and I had studied with him and my sissy for hours. But when it came to quiz time, I couldn't give them the same answer I had previously given them. It was as if my mind was blank. They thought I was just nervous because I had to stand in front of him, but that wasn't the case. Well, I was a little nervous because he's a walking being of knowledge. He's like a genius. I was so ashamed and afraid to tell him the real reason I couldn't remember.

Not in a million years had I ever thought a day would come, and I would have to reveal one of the darkest and defining moments of my life to anyone. I never imagine sharing such darkness and shame from my past, especially with a person who I'd honored and cherished so much. To talk to him about one of the most defining traumatic moments that changed the entire trajectory of my life. At this moment, Time feels like it has come to a pause; this conversation can not happen. I was so nervous as if I was

13

Cinderella standing on the ballroom floor, afraid that when the clock strikes midnight, he will see the broken side of me. The woman who got transformed because God waved his magical grace wand over her life. The hands of the father have healed my outer scars, so I wouldn't look like what I've been through. I was afraid to reveal that part of my past.

I was ashamed of, and honestly, I did not want to relive the story. I couldn't form my words, and my palms were sweating, my body felt as if I was going to pass out. "Oh, GOD, Why me?" Was my prayer and thought. I wanted him to never look at me as weak or a victim. I wanted him to love the mother I was, the entrepreneur, the visionary, and all the great things about God. I respected his opinion of me. I wanted him to know the woman I had become, not the victim of domestic violence I've had to live through.

There are some moments that are ordained by the father to help you heal while being restored. You have to be willing to embrace them; this was my moment. It's amazing what fear will make you think about yourself. The funny part is that I had written a whole book centered around just about everything I was afraid to say to him personally, and the world had read it! Wow! So here I go, I took a deep breath, he's sitting right next to me, and I revealed to him about a past relationship many years ago, how the man I was with physically abused me. From putting a knife to my neck to slicing my fingers when I tried to stop him from cutting my throat to beating me unconsciously, and the effect of the blows to my head and the trauma has affected my short term and long term memories for

14

years. I had to sit there facing him, like an onion I had to peel layer by layer the reason I could not retain hours of studying to this man whom I had prayed would not only still loved me but see me. What was once one of my greatest fears became a place of comfort and healing. The shedding became the freedom and breakthrough needed for me to trust all of me with him. I learned that day what real love looks like and feels like, what being safe felt like and what trust really was. I realize that day; if you want to know if you're in love with a person, you'll know when you're willing to become naked before them about what makes you afraid, what hurts you and when you can share with them your heart that still needs to be mended.

Again, fear will hold you hostage of what could happen that might not ever come to pass. My fear was if I speak of my horrible past, my future wouldn't look at me the same or worst, that I would have to live the next few hours or days or even years pretending I was ok. In this past domestic violence, I laid there for three days from been beaten unrecognizable and going in and out of consciousness. The blows to my head caused short term & long term memory loss, and for the rest of my life I will struggle to remember and suffer from terrible Migraine headaches.

Whew! To share this with him felt as if my heart was about to burst out of my chest, tears rolled down my face, and when I looked at him, tears rolled down his face too. He held me in his arms and said to me, "I'm so sorry," but Bae, you will never have to experience that ever again." And from that day until time past he would protect me from the pain of it by not even allowing certain scenes on Tv because he said he never wanted me to have to witness or have to revisit that place. The beauty of this love was; as a whole woman with some scars, I wasn't looking for him to complete me but accept me completely. His non-judgmental love for me and his ability to listen to my soul became the catalyst of change for the inner awakening of a displaced perspective once viewed by myself. This moment in time caused a domino effect. My personal philosophy regarding the cultural behavior of the male gender and their sensitivity towards women was suddenly dismantled. I had experienced the epitome of unconditional love like never before. He loved me through the fear of shame.

As humans, our greatest fear is the fear of being judged. We are judged about our very own truth. Can you imagine being imperfect and being judged by an imperfect world? Wow! But because it matters to you what the imperfect think about you, you sit on the sidelines of your dreams, afraid of people who will never get in the game and Scared of people who will never be able to tell your story, people who will never know what it takes just to be you. Many people are so scared of starting a new relationship because judging people know you have been divorced. You unconsciously become scared by people who will always have enough boldness to share their opinions of what you should and should not do, and the very advice they are giving is an opinion to a life they have never lived. It is absolutely mind-boggling how a person who has never walked by faith can tell you your faith will never work. The very person who has lived in the same apartment for years has a genius idea about the risk of homeownership; however, they have never taken the necessary steps to buy a home, but they have all the advice of why its a bad idea for others. Now, I'm not sure which has me baffled, the fact that they have an opinion regarding the subject or the fact that people actually listen to them and take their advice! I believe most people that try to talk you out of becoming a greater you operate in a level of self-defeat, self-sabotage and fear. But as dreamers or a visionary, when you find yourself in the transformation of life where it appears destiny is pulling to walk by faith and not by sight, you will know its destiny pulling because you have an inner belief and knowing that your life has more to offer you and the world than where you are now. Moving past fear and the opinion of others will persuade you to pursue your purpose. It will introduce you to the person you have never met but destined to become. There is a you that you have not met yet. My advice is to close a deaf ear to the voices of people who are talking but are not saying anything. They have no evidence of success from a failure, no facts of a give up to a comeback but only fruitless conversation of a lifeless seed never to be sown into the earth that truthfully spoken is the real proof and testament of a person who's fear has more substance in their life than faith.

Have you ever gone to a football game, and everyone is cheering for the home team? But you have that one individual who knows more about the game than anyone else? They know more than the paid individuals who have proven records of accomplishments and experience; he yells at the coach as to what the coach is doing wrong. He screams from the bleachers what the team and players should be doing and not doing. He huffs and puffs and blows and pouts because no one that is in the game is listening to him for advice. The truth is, he's only played the game on an Xbox ! He's never been on a field and has never been a coach. But he is the xbox 360 champion of football, and he considers himself an expert of the game because he has the highest score on all pro football 2019, he has a player's mentality which says his perspective of the game can be one-sided. However, the funny thing is, he's sitting in the bleachers in a real stadium, but in his little world, he is the NFL coach of all time. However, in real life, he's not even on the sideline as a paid advisor! What's wrong with this Picture? What I am saying to you is; there will always be people on the sidelines giving you advice on how to walk on water but have never themselves gotten out of the boat. A wise being should take counsel from the person who has proven to have tried it and failed big just to bounce back to become successful. You can always find them in the game of life making plays. It's your time to get in the game, you have practiced long enough.

Fear is like any other emotion. We just give it more power

RELENTLESS THE NEW FEAR

Being transparent about who you are is revealing to the eyes and hearts of judgmental people what it took for you to be who you are, showing to them that you are living in the truth of YOU. It is not the Dare, but the challenge. As long as you can sit and rest in the hope of a thing, it is a safe but frustrating place of comfort that's married to Complacency. You are more than the fear you feel.

For those that are finding themselves in a repetitive cycle or you may feel as if you are stuck in life in certain areas, it is time for you to confront the areas of your life that are causing you to feel defeated. The areas that are making you feel broken and lost. You have to confront and deal with the areas of your life that you feel you have failed or have not been as successful as you would like, and lastly, you must be willing to face the truth and deal with it without making excuses while holding yourself accountable. You have to realize that your greatest fear is not with what you see, but what you will not confront.

I had to realize that you have to have people in your life or a person in your corner that will help you in being relentless while confronting these areas. Sometimes you need a voice of agreement. Sometimes you need that extra push to keep going even when things look hopeless. Sometimes you need someone in your sphere of influence that will be able to shed a different light on what's dark in your life because many times, we are willing to tell the truth to others about themselves but will not tell ourselves the truth. we will run from the reality about ourselves.

I can recall so vividly a season of my life when it appeared to me my whole life was in transition. From family and finances to Business and ministry. I felt, and I found myself with more questions than answers that only God could give. Many times you can experience life & find yourself in a feeling of despair. Life can hit you so hard and throw you a curveball until you don't know which way is up. I remember the day when life hit me so hard; all I could do was cry. I was in a dark place, and it felt as if the walls were closing in on me. I could not get out of bed, I did not want to leave my house, I did not want to talk to anyone nor see anyone and my vision of who I was and the life I had once lived were no more. My vision and hope for a better day had become so blurred until I no longer saw purpose. I could no longer see my way out of this cave I was in. Yes, the Evangelist, the motivational speaker, the one that others call on to pray for them, she couldn't even pray for herself at this point. I had no words to pray, no strength, and no momentum. Have you ever been there? Have you ever found yourself in the crossroads of life? Maybe after a loved one passed away or you had experienced a major life change, possibly a divorce or the loss of a job, the death of a child, or a traumatic incident or accident. But whatever the case may be, it had become like a mountain in your life that appeared too hard to go over, or a valley that seems to feel as if it was swallowing you up of like a grave of quicksand. No one really ever wants to admit that they too, have been there; in a low place, especially when people accustomed to you being the go-to person. Isn't it amazing the people that were with you when everything seemed well, to disappear when things go south? I have many people that love me and some that have been in my life for years. But on this particular day, I remember I could not stop crying, I remember lying on my bedroom floor in a fatal position and crying out to God from the depth of my soul ."where are you'?!!. All I knew to do was to holla "help me" !! because the pain was too much to bear. Not even 10 mins passed and my phone began to ring, the Lord sent a voice of comfort, strength, and trust by way of a close sister and friend, who I call Sissy. She began to speak life into the soul that had become weary and broken, she began to pray for me, but she also reminded me of who God said I am and would become. It's not like anyone else had not spoken those words to me, but that day, at that moment in time, her voice was the CPR and life support to bring me back to life. It's amazing how God knows who you need at the right time, She was not only the sister I needed, but she reveal the heart of a person who did not judge my low place. I will forever be grateful for the love between us that only God knew was designed just for me. Oprah has her Gale, Lavern has Shirley, Mork had Mindy, And Melissa has Cindy Paul hill.

It is my prayer as you overcome the spirit of fear that the Lord will send you too your Johnathan connection. (reference 1 Samuel 18:3) This bond or divine relationship is someone that is equipped to pray, carry, handle, love, support, push correct, and at times cry with you, but what makes this relationship so very much Divine is that: this relationship is mutually beneficial to you both. It's not just

21

one-sided, but the two are reciprocators of love, grace, and so much more.; this is someone that will not judge you, but give you a jump start to your next level.

MAKE FEAR YOUR FUEL

My fear was to be loved.

My fear was poverty.

My fear was not being good enough.

My fear was not becoming who they said I should be.

My fear was not meeting my expectations because I had no one else but me.

My fear was not measuring up.

My fear was hurting someone because life hurts people.

My fear was knowing my truth but scared of living or facing it.

My Fear was removing the mask I put on just to be strong enough to look in the mirror.

, to be ordinary or average when I didn't like Mediocrity.

My fear was facing THEM and THEY.

Fear is now my My FUEL to LIVE FEARLESSLY.

Join me.

She thought she could fly, so she did, only to find out
***SOARING** was Easier.*

*She just needed to spread her wings, and the wind would do
the rest.*

CHAPTER 2

SHADARIA ALLISON

You, The Doctor, The Midwife, and The Patient

Congratulations! You've made it past triage and into the birthing room. Ready or not, we are having a baby. The doctor is here to deliver the baby. The midwife is present to help the patient give birth to the baby, and the patient is ready to push. There is just one last quintessential detail to finish out this birthing process; it's time to determine your place in the room. Are you the doctor? The experienced professional that knows how to accomplish deliverance. Are you the midwife? The wise counsel skilled to urge the patient during the process of birth. Maybe you are the patient representing the signal of a shift that will change lives forever. If you're not sure, it is ok. You are not alone. I want to welcome you on a journey with me. Together, we can determine where you are. The Doctor, The biggest expectation from the doctor to the patient, is an experience. During the birthing process, everyone wants to be found in the hands of a tenured professional. Someone that either has a track record of successful deliveries or one that has even themselves gone through the process of birth. The doctor is usually the most trusted person during the birthing process, as well. Their expertise, education, and the ability to deliver a healthy baby create room for the assuredness needed on everyone's behalf to harness a successful birthing environment. Without the doctor, all who stand in the birthing room are in grave danger. The role of a doctor comes at an enormous cost. One must have had to have studied for many years, proving themselves qualified while being able to withstand multiple phases of crucial testing (often for years on end), eventually producing a sharp sense of discernment and the dynamic wisdom required to facilitate optimum health. Think about it. Would you want an inexperienced doctor delivering your most prized possession? Probably not. It is for that reason that you may now awaken to your place in the birthing room. Many of us may be doctors without knowing it.

During the fall of 2018, I was asked to write a thesis on my educational objective towards earning a doctoral degree in the field of political science. One of my lifelong dreams was to obtain an honorary doctorate. The distinction between a regular doctorate and an honorary doctoral degree is its acquisition. One requires formal education, and the other requires an election based on the evidence of a profound success in the knowledge of theory, contribution(s) to society, or by reward/merit. Earning an honorary doctorate would mean that though I didn't attain the doctoral status by normal or traditional means, my EXPERIENCE would still qualify me for the same title, accolade, benefit, and accommodation. I lived my life in what I'd like to call "C&C,"

cycles and circles. For a long time, it seemed as if I'd never get out of some "life test." It was like I couldn't lose an apartment once; I had to lose it three times. I couldn't be with an abusive man once; I had to be with four. I couldn't wreck the car of my life once. I had to self-sabotage for many years until I found myself in a circular cycle of events that would eventually make me an expert. It was under many trials and indefinite error that I realized I was becoming not more of a problem, but rather the solution to someone else's. God was developing a practitioner in me. I was becoming a doctor. Signs You May Be the Doctor: Your life has been extremely tough. You have had to both face and fight most of your darkest battles alone. You often cycle between risk and reward. You witness, withstand, and survive painful opposition. Your latter years have been phenomenal or showed drastic contrast from your past. You often experience droplets of breakthrough and not waves because the lessons learned must be intricately woven into the pattern of your life. You have mastered at least one "problem" area of your life and have been able to monetize it or gain success from it. People trust your leadership. Okay doctor, now that we know who you are, wash your hands, check your patients' vitals, and let's get ready to help birth a baby.

The Midwife There is no "step-down" as it pertains to the ranking of expertise inside of the birthing room. The levels of need and importance are typically based on emergency and often more by the moment. Birthing can begin as a steady paced event and quickly change into swift action; this is the primary reason that Midwives are especially needed before, during, and after the delivery. The midwife may have more vested during the birthing process of the coming baby than any other outward participant. I like to think of the midwife as the "pastor" of the birthing room. They are not only astronomically equipped to help birth, but they are also vital caretakers of the patient and the baby. Long before the doctor or any other staff hits the birthing room, the midwife more-than-likely, knows more about the patient than any other health care professional and may have even developed a deep bond with the patient. In the birthing room, the midwife's duties vary in operation.

Midwives are usually present to educate the patient on what to expect during labor, administer medication, and, more importantly, provide emotional support to the laboring patient. Where the doctor may only be acquainted with the statistic of the patient, the midwife is acquainted with the person of the patient. Where the doctor may not be called upon until it's time for the patient to give birth, the midwife is called to the patient's period. Truth be told, if all went "down in flames," midwives, though often coined as "the help," maybe equipped with enough wisdom. Should duty call, to step into the role of the doctor and deliver the baby, themselves. Many of us may be midwives without knowing it. I sat hunched over a toilet on a warm day in the summer of 2007. By this time, I had taken the second pill from planned parenthood, and the small cramps, I was advised that I'd feel from this medical abortion had now left me with a pale face, tons of blood loss, and a yolky sac afloat rouge-tinted toilet water. I needed an ambulance. At just 20 years old, already an impoverished mother of one three-year-old toddler, I knew nothing but survival. An ambulance was outside of my survival budget. The friend I was living with at the time heard my whimpering from the bathroom and determining it was worth her attention, she and her then-boyfriend got dressed and took me to the nearest emergency room. With tear-filled eyes looking at the IV pumps, feeling almost faint in a hospital emergency bed, I reached for my cell phone and called my mentor from church. It had only been one year from my 19th birthday, almost one year into her mentorship program, and two weeks after, she advised me not to get the abortion that we had spoken. "I do not support abortion Shadaria," She said. "However, I do support you, and whatever decision you make, I will be there for you." The memory of our last conversations almost snatched my voice as I tried to express my current emergency to her. Keeping her word, she showed up to the hospital, not to midwife my birth, but to midwife my shame.

Signs you May Be the Midwife: Your life has been extremely tough. You have had to both face and fight most of your darkest battles alone. You are the first notified in the time of trouble. You are the one that others strongly rely on for help. You have a keen gift of "exhortation." Even when you are broken, you help mend the hearts of others. You have a devout prayer life. You have a strong unction to serve the world around you. You are extremely compassionate. Okay, Midwife, now that we know who you are, wash your hands, check your patients' emotions, vitals, and let's get ready to help birth a baby. The Patient: While administering birth, the experience qualifies the doctor, the wisdom qualifies the midwife, but the pressure qualifies the patient. While it may seem that life is about having the credentials of the doctor and the wit of the midwife, the most important and most valued participant in the birthing room considerably is the patient. The patient doesn't have to be uninformed. She doesn't have to have it all together, she doesn't have to come from wealth, neither is she expected to know the mysteries of medical jargon. Yet, in every facet of her existence, the patient is the prize. The doctor and the midwife have been blessings to the patient. However, what she is pregnant with is a blessing to the world. Her body has been stretched beyond human capacity. She has been the host of a life she does not yet know. She has had to be conscious of what she eats, what she drinks, and what she allows into her system. Her life has and is about to change forever. She isn't allowed to succumb to any fear she once had about life or death. She has been mandated to carry and prepped to deliver. Whether she feels ready about it all or not, she is about to give birth by any means necessary. Many of us may be patients without knowing it. I drove around the city of Birmingham for hours in my friend's car. I made several stops amongst familiar places. Surprisingly, no one had me locked up. My hair unraveled on the top of my head. My make-up smeared, and my speech laced with the traits of one who had no real attachment to either God or sanity.

"I'm going to be a billionaire," I told a random Walmart cashier.

"You are Jesus," I told my son.

It was August 24, 2012, on my son's 8th birthday when I lost all grips with reality. A product of an affair, a troubled childhood, molestation, an unstable life, homelessness, abuse, teen-pregnancy, generational curses, and despair. I guess the question was: how long did I expect myself to go on living in dysfunctional forms of "normal" before I lost my natural mind? By the grace of God, I never saw the inside of a mental facility. I was blessed to be surrounded by prayer warriors who knew me well enough to know what to do. I spent almost two hours undergoing a high level of deliverance. It was one of the most traumatic experiences I have had to date.

At 25 years old, raised in church all my life, a leader in the choir, and "born again," I was mentally ill and oppressed by the demons of my "undealt-with" past. As I came, I remember a friend of mine being present and saying, "Shadaria, I drew a picture as the music was playing, and everybody was praying for you." My mind had taken all I could absorb. My pride was exploited by embarrassment, and my heart ripped to shreds wondering why God allowed this moment to happen to me at all. After all, I felt I had gone through enough. My tear-filled eyes turned their attention to my friend as he showed me the portrait he made for me, a colored picture of 'Jesus' eye encompassed by tears. It wasn't until I did an interview on Fox Television in 2017, after writing my fifth book petitioning faith-based communities, health care professionals, and state legislators to consider revamping an abandoned hospital site into a state of the art rehab and recreational facility for the mentally ill, impoverished, and drug-addicted individuals that I realized I was the patient. It was at that moment I realized that I went through all those things to birth out my life's calling. Signs that you may be the patient: your life has been extremely tough. You have had to both face and fight most of your darkest battles alone. You question your existence. You feel you were born for more. You face uncertainty about your identity. You are anointed. You have been gravely misunderstood by others, especially family. You wish to know God on a deeper level. You are extremely creative. You have extreme favor on your life and have been prophetically confirmed as being anointed. Okay, patient, now that we know who you are, breathe. Let's get ready to birth a baby. The birthing room can be compared to life or "life's stage." Depending on its severity, we can often question our place in the room. Are we the doctor? The decorated professional able to discern the fragment of someone else's pain and know where to find a solution that leads to deliverance. Are we midwives? The seasoned exhorter who can reflect on our personal story and troubles to help someone else deliver their blessing or be delivered from their disappointment. Are we the patient? The valuable prize, pregnant with something that will change who we are, while blessing the world around us. The amazing thing about being any of these key participants is this: no matter where you stand in the birthing room, you stand in alignment with the path that moves according to the gifts and the call of God on your life. There is no one stage more important than the other as eventually, you may find yourself simultaneously occupying them all. Understand that everything that was brought up against your life was refinement for the "golden seed" planted within you by God. That seed is his word. Consider the biggest, tallest, and oldest tree you have ever seen. It started with a seed. Over time, that tree endured tornadoes, storms, and possible erosions, only to still rise above the ground, remaining rooted, outliving the opposition. So, I say to you today, wherever and whoever you are in the "birthing room," Doctor, suit up. Midwife, boot up. Patient, bear down and push. Ready or not, we are having a baby.

CHAPTER 3

APRIL VAUGHN

WRITINGS ON THE WALLS

"Before I formed you in the womb I knew you,
and before you were born I consecrated you;
I appointed you a prophet to the nations."– Jeremiah 1:5

I've often wondered what those moments were like with my Heavenly Father; before I entered into the life that I know now. The moment when He set me apart, when the whispers of His familiar voice fell faintly on my fetal ears, nearly drowned out by the sound of screams and crashing pieces of shattered dreams echoing in my mother's womb. Utterances meant just for me. He etched them on the walls of my heart. In a place that no one or nothing could touch, where they would remain waiting for me to find them at the appointed time.

"For I know the plans I have for you, declares the Lord,
plans to prosper you and not to harm you, plans to give you
hope and a future.– Jeremiah 29:11

On April 16, in the year 1982, I was born. Almost a full month past my expected due date, I was a hefty 9 lbs. 10 oz. and "2 feet tall" - as my mother used to say. As a kid, I remember she and my aunts joking that I was so big that I "walked right out of the womb." We laugh at it now, but the atmosphere in the delivery room was one of panic and worry. My mother's small frame couldn't handle the stress of giving birth to a baby my size; so, the doctor had to perform an emergency cesarean. Thank God that all went well, and at 10:28 pm that Friday night my story began.

I'd like to be able to say that the circumstances surrounding my arrival were picture-perfect; and that the hospital halls were filled with family and friends waiting to welcome me, but that just wasn't my reality. My mother, a 16-year-old high school junior, had gone nearly six months into her pregnancy without anyone even knowing I existed. It was her basketball coach that eventually noticed a change in her weight and called a meeting with my grandmother to let her know that she couldn't allow my mother to play in the Christmas tournament because she was with child. I can't imagine what my mother was feeling, star athlete and honor roll student, one year from graduation, multiple academic and athletic scholarships hanging in the wings, now a single teen mother (long before it could land you a lucrative spot on reality TV). Her life as she knew it was changed forever. My grandmother, although married to my grandfather at the time, had her first child as an unwed teen, and the cycle was repeating. And to make bad worse, my mother (still a child herself) was bringing home a newborn without the support or involvement of my father.

"Talitha koum!" ("Little Girl Arise!") – Mark 5:41

I thank God that my grandparents were there to help. They came from very humble beginnings but did pretty well for themselves, considering neither of them graduated from high school. My grandfather landed a job with General Motors, and my grandmother attended night school to get her medical coding certification and worked for the hospital where both I and my mother were born. Being that my mother was the youngest of eight and the last in the house, my grandparents ("Big Ma" and "Big Daddy" as I affectionately called them) became more like my parents.

I could say that if it weren't for them, I don't know where I'd be, but that would be a lie. I know EXACTLY where I'd be...dead. That's because when I was just an infant, my heart stopped. My grandmother found me in my crib limp, lifeless, and turning pale in the face. She grabbed me up, screamed for my grandfather, and they rushed me to the hospital. When telling the story, my grandmother would always emphasize how fast my grandfather got us to the emergency room. "He drove like a bat out of hell!" she'd say with a chuckle and a smile. "One minute we were leaving home, and the next minute we were there!" I believe his "Dukes of Hazard" driving could have very well been what saved my life because the doctors were able to revive me without incident.

Unfortunately, that was not the last time I'd be carried (or walk) through hospital doors. Before I was a year old, I was back again. This time for my first surgery, to remove a cyst that had grown to

35

the size of a golf ball in my throat. I was so young that I don't remember it at all, but I carry a scar across the front of my neck that won't let me forget it. The next time I had surgery, I was about 4 or 5 years old, and I remember it like it was yesterday. I was having excruciating abdominal pain caused by a spastic bladder and had to be put under anesthesia for cystoscopy and expansion.

I had been back and forth to Egleston Children's Hospital countless times, trying to figure out what the problem was. My mother and I were there so much that I knew exactly where to go, what button to push on the elevator, and where to look on the Medicaid card to get them the information they needed to check us in. The waiting room and play area were always filled with children who were sick or crying in pain. I would always ask my mother "What's wrong with them…what have they done? Are they here for the same thing I'm here for???" I believe it was during this time that my dream of becoming a pediatrician began. I was fascinated with the diagrams and charts on the walls. I was always rummaging through the drawers in the exam rooms and asking the nurses and doctors a-million-and-one questions.

On the night of my surgery, I recall reading the pamphlet over and over with my mother making sure I knew exactly what they were going to do, what the tools looked like if I'd feel anything, how long I would be put under, and how they would wake me up. I was terrified, but my desire to stop the pain was greater than my fear. Little did I know it was in this time in my life that I would get to know a different kind of pain, the type that's not physical, but hurts just the same. Maybe even more.

The Lord is near to the brokenhearted and saves the crushed in spirit.- Psalm 34:18

By this time, my mother had had my first sister (who was just one year younger than I), moved out from my grandparents' house into an apartment on the other side of town, and we were living with her boyfriend. Their relationship was like a roller. They would be partying and laughing one minute and fighting like cats and dogs the next. We'd spend nights in the rural parts of town playing outside of abandoned buildings, where the ground was covered with used drug needles, while they drank and smoked weed with friends around the fire barrel, racing cars and motorcycles up and down the street. It seemed like every time we got home there was something to fight about. One night it got scarier, and I was afraid that my mother was going to get hurt; so, I stepped in between them, thinking that there was no way he would hurt me. He flung me like a rag doll into the glass patio door, and I, along with my childish naivety, fell to the floor, and my spirit was crushed.

My eyes were instantly opened to a world that I had not known. My world, as I knew it was shattered. Hurt, pain, and uncertainty had spilled over into and tainted my perception of love, protection, and stability. Other than my grandfather, he was the only father figure that I remember in my life at the time. (There are pictures of me at my grandmother's house at earlier ages, but I have no recollection of spending any time with my "real" dad or that side of

37

my family before the age of about 6 or 7). He was the one that I saw day in and day out, the one that dropped me off on my first day of kindergarten and assured me that he and my mother would be there to get me off of the bus when the school day was over. (I had extreme separation anxiety because my mother was consistently late picking us up from daycare, and my sister and I would always be the last two there.) And now I saw him in a completely new light. Things were different now, and it only got worse.

I remember getting off of the bus one day and walking all the way to our building all by myself because my mother wasn't at the bus stop to walk me home. As soon as I entered the doors on the bottom floor, I heard the screams of a woman. They were faint at first, but the closer I got to our floor; I realized that it was my mother. Backpack in tow, I ran up the stairs to our apartment, and the door was wide open. He was chasing my mother around the coffee table with a butcher's knife. I begged and pleaded for him to stop but to no avail. I ran to our neighbor's for help, and the police were called. Thank God that my mother was not killed, but she stayed.

A month or so later, my second sister was born. I used to hang out next to her bassinet swing in the living room watching over her like a hawk. I'd cover her ears while she slept, so the yelling and screaming wouldn't startle her. The fighting was getting worse, and the alcohol and weed had progressed to cocaine. I vividly recall pouring a pixie stick on the living room table and snorting it through the paper wrapper after seeing them snort lines off a mirror. I felt like my whole face was on fire and my eyes and nose were watering profusely. I told my mother what happened and I got the worst whooping of my life. In my mind, the intense burning that I felt in my nostrils should have been punishment enough.

Then there was a shift, I didn't know exactly what it was then, but I knew that the smell was different. It was very distinct, like melted plastic with a hint of sweetness. Soda and beer cans became a coveted commodity, and not for recycling. My sister and I would find them all over the place, bent, riddled with pinholes, and covered with burnt ashes. Being in the house was like being on an episode of "The Walking Dead." They'd creep around, wide-eyed, peeping through the curtains telling us to be quiet so they could listen to see if someone was coming. They were present but absent at the same time. So, we learned to do for ourselves. As a 5-year-old, I was washing bottles, mixing formula, and changing my little sister's diapers. I was forced to grow up well before my time.

To save you, I will send an army. – Isaiah 43:14

It was such a relief when their relationship finally ended. I remember feeling like my grandfather was my savior when he pulled up in his baby blue and white Ford pick-up truck to help us pack up all of our stuff. I felt safe when he was around. Like no one or nothing could touch us. We were leaving all of the chaos and craziness behind and getting a new start.

We moved to the projects, and life was far from easy, but for a moment, we had peace. I have a fond memory of dancing on the table with my sister while my mother decorated the Christmas tree. We'd picked up a large black garbage bag full of toys from the Salvation Army, and we were excited to have gifts under the tree. I liked it when it was just us. We didn't have a lot, but we had each other.

My mother was still battling addiction and struggled to hold a steady job. So, we never stayed anywhere long. She registered us for school with my grandparents' address, so that was always consistent which was good because I loved school. I was placed in the gifted program in kindergarten and because I excelled in academics all of my teachers loved me. The school became my haven. But we spent the next few years bouncing around from place to place. We went from apartments to a few months with one boyfriend, here and another couple of months with the next boyfriend there. We slept in motel rooms for a night or two at a time, on a blowup mattress at my grandparents', then on a daybed in my aunt's living room. By this time my mother had my baby sister, so it was five of us in one bed. Most of the time, my first sister and I slept on a pallet on the floor. Nowhere ever felt like home.

We moved to this one place that I will never forget. It was an apartment converted from an old college dorm. The beds were built-in and the rooms were cramped with no windows. At night you could hear the rats crawling over each other in the walls. I was

40

always afraid to fall asleep or get up in the middle of the night to go to the bathroom. It was just the five of us initially, then, one of her boyfriends moved in with us, and things took a quick turn for the worst. They would drink and get high daily. One night they got into an argument about what who knows, and the fight escalated. My sisters and I heard banging, crashing, and clashing from our room and came running to help. There was blood everywhere! She had stabbed him during the altercation and was on the phone calling 911. Because the police were on the way, he ran. The oldest of my three younger sisters and I helped my mother clean up blood from the floor, and the furniture before the police arrived so that she wouldn't be taken to jail. We had visited my uncles in prison many times before, and I couldn't imagine my mother being in a place like that. Little did I know there would come a time where I wouldn't have to imagine it because it soon became a reality.

As one whom his mother comforts, so I will comfort you.
Isaiah 66:13

To make extra money, put clothes on our back, and food on the table; my mother became a booster. Stealing became the norm. Whenever she put on biking pants and her oversized blue jean dress or brought the "big purse," I knew exactly what was about to happen. She would have us stand around her and the shopping cart while she stuffed clothes, food, household goods, and whatever else would fit in her pants. I hated it, It gave me so much anxiety because I knew deep down it was wrong. I eventually started refusing to stand guard and would tell her to take everything out and put it back, and so, she started making me stay in the car. She was arrested a couple of times and spent no more than a few weeks in jail, but for me it seemed like an eternity. My sisters and I would all crowd around the mustard yellow rotary dial phone on the wall in my grandparents' kitchen to take our turn talking to her before going to bed. Even though we were living with my grandparents, I felt a huge responsibility to take care of my sisters while she was gone.

Then came a time when it felt like we didn't have a care in the world. My mother began dating a man we called "Cat," and EVERYTHING changed. He was the first person I'd ever seen that had a phone in his car. He was always dressed to the nines (even if we were just spending the day in the park) and lavishly adorned with jewelry, a gold watch with diamonds, diamond rings, gold chains, and we too had new clothes, new shoes, new furniture, and an actual house to put it in. We didn't just get beds; we got bunk beds that looked like a house with a slide (a little girl's dream)! I no longer felt anxious going shopping with my mother. She always had a wad of cash and bought us any and everything we needed or wanted. Every day was like Christmas! But things were not as good as they seemed.

I began to notice small things like there were always strange people coming to the house. My mother would be "cooking," but we'd be forbidden from entering the kitchen. We'd see rows and rows of gallon-sized freezer bags in the cabinet filled with weed. I was about nine years old at the time but was very keen. I was always listening in on "grown folks' conversations" and recognized that something wasn't right. And not too long after, it all came to my head. The police raided the house, and my mother went to jail...again.

She bonded out, but the charges she was facing were much more serious than shoplifting. We moved back with my grandparents, who were furious and fed up. The charges were somehow reduced, and she got off with five years of probation; this meant she had to be clean for FIVE YEARS, So she had to go to rehab. I knew what that meant because my grandfather had gone a time or two for alcoholism. He was the pillar of our family but would go through bouts of binge drinking where he'd become someone else, someone very belligerent and careless. We were only in elementary school, but he'd force us to drink tall cans of Budweiser, and smoke joints rolled up in newspaper. (For that reason, I can't stand the taste of beer to this day!)

I just didn't understand why my mother couldn't just stop??? Did she not know the hell and shame we would go through being the black sheep of the family? Now she'd be leaving us to basically fend for ourselves for months. My sisters and I sat at her feet weeping and sobbing as she packed her bags to leave. It seemed like it took forever to get there, but it still wasn't enough time. We dropped her off, said our goodbyes, and on the way home I gazed out of the window with tears streaming down my face as Patti LaBelle's "Somebody Loves You Baby" played on the radio. I was feeling so alone and overwhelmed with the thoughts of everything that had happened, was happening, and was going to happen, but as soon as that song came on, I felt like God was wrapping His arms around me, letting me know that everything was going to be okay.

> **The Lord himself goes before you and will be with you; he will never leave you nor forsake you. Do not be afraid; do not be discouraged.– Deuteronomy 31:8**

Everything was not okay. It was actually a lot more of the same over and over again, but I was comforted in knowing that God was with me.

- When my mother went back and forth to rehab,
  He was with me.
- When my father was in and out of my life and jail,
  He was with me.
- When I frantically called my grandmother at work, afraid my mother was going to die from the pills she took to take her life,
  He was with me.
- When my mother would leave for weeks at a time and left me to care for my three sisters,
  He was with me.
- When my grandparents threatened to put us out, and I was frantically calling anyone I knew to take us into no avail,
  He was with me.

- When I walked across the stage with honors at my high school graduation with not a single family member in the audience,

  He was with me.

- When I nearly lost my life at the hands of someone my mother called a friend,

  He was with me.

- When I narrowly escaped death in a hit and run car accident,

  He was with me.

- When I had to find the courage to take the stand and face the man that tried to take my life,

  He was with me.

- When I withdrew from college to recover from my injuries and PTSD, and everyone told me I would never go back and finish,

  He was with me.

- When I went back and became the first on BOTH sides of my family to earn a college degree,

  HE WAS WITH ME!

And my story is far from over. There are generations and nations that stand to benefit from the assignments that He has given me to fulfill. There is no sickness, no struggle, no setback, no attack, and no adversity that can stop me! The promises that He made to me long before I was even a thought remain written on the walls of my heart and will be with me always, and I will walk in my God-given authority conquering every mountain that stands in my way because He is with me! And he is with you!!

CHAPTER 4

KAREN BEVERLY

TURNING POINT

Turning point-a time at which a decisive change in a situation occurs, especially one with beneficial results.

I have always loved to sing and perform.

I was in a singing group called Tomboy since I was 13 years old. The group consisted of 5 girls. We all went to a theater program together called Playmakers at Howard University. One of our teachers there decided to put a singing group together. He handpicked us! After the group was formed, we became like sisters. We spent so much time together rehearsing for shows, performing, and hanging out. One of the girls was in middle school; the rest of us were in High school. I went to Suitland High, a performing arts school.

I auditioned and was accepted into their music program. I took eight classes a day — all my regular academic classes and then music classes. Two of the extracurricular activities I participated in were chorus and the gospel choir. Even though it was extra It was my passion, and passion never feels like work.

During this time in my life, I was so excited about being apart of this amazing group with such awesome young ladies who love to sing just as much as I. It's so surprising that I was so wrapped up in my passion of singing that I was so shocked when something else got my attention. It was a guy!!!

I met my daughter's father in my 11th-grade year, and I was madly in love.

We were together every second, and he even picked me up after school, so I didn't have to ride the school bus home. It felt like we had the perfect relationship.

I knew we were going to get married and live happily ever after.

A year after we started dating, I got pregnant; this was a major turning point in my life.

I was scared to death. Did I say that correctly? Let me repeat this. I was scared to death to the funeral home to the grave! I knew when I saw the results I was DOA!! Dead on arrival! That means when it comes the time to tell my parents, one of us was going to need CPR. And that would be me, the teenage pregnant girl. I am checking my pulse because I had told my parents we weren't having sex, so I had a lot of explaining to do. And how do you get pregnant without having sex? How do I explain this? It's not like my name was Mary and Joseph and I'm Carrying the christ! Boy at that time, I wish I was, and I could have blamed it all on the holy spirit, shucks even Casper was a thought.

I didn't know what to do!

I called my child's father and told him I thought I was pregnant. Even though we were best friends and in love, I didn't know what his reaction would be. Thankfully he was very supportive, even though he was scared too, he wasn't upset at all. He told me I should take a test. I took 3! I wanted one of them to be negative so I kept taking them. They all said the same thing. I was shocked. In English it all said positive! For some reason I never thought this would happen to me. How ironic, I had always looked down on girls who got pregnant in high school. I know that wasn't right, but I did. Who would allow themselves to be in such shame and embarrassment to be a teenage mom? Because quite frankly if you were pregnant that means everyone would now know you are sexually active! And who would be dumb enough to reveal what's really going on in your teenage world, well, I guess I fell into the big reveal category, and of all the days, I was going out of town with my singing group this particular morning I took the tests. I was struggling emotionally between the reality of being pregnant and what I thought my destiny was. Don't get me wrong, I loved my boyfriend very much but I also really wanted to travel and sing when I graduated. This Turning point has changed the Trajectory of my life! What am I to do?

I wanted to just go out of town and not deal with the situation, but I couldn't. I knew I had to stay home and talk to my parents.

49

So I didn't go. I'm now having to be the big girl and face this big girl's problem. First, I had to tell my mom and dad. Jesus, take the wheel!! I was more afraid to tell my mom because she was always the disciplinarian. I thought she would not only be angry but very disappointed in me, but for some strange reason, my mom's reaction was different than I thought it would be. Even though she was extremely disappointed she was very calm and asked me what I wanted to do. I could not believe it! She was calm which honestly made me more terrified! How can she be composed in a time like this? Knowing how she has raised me to be a respectable daughter and she trusted me to be smarter than my current actions were revealing. On the other hand, my dad was the one I thought would be more understanding because even though he was definitely the head of the house, he had a real soft spot for his girls, but of course my dad was not happy at all, he was the one angry. He even asked me whose baby it was. Drop the mic! Pose that question to me again, dad? Umm, what? Who's baby is it?

As if he thought I was sleeping around with a lot of people. I felt so hurt that the person I looked up to the most was now looking down on me. I was astonished that because of this situation he would question my character. I could not believe, first of all, I'm pregnant; secondly, my mom was utterly not herself and thirdly my dad has just labeled me and not with the title of a daughter. I am beyond angry at myself and to put the icing on the cake; this moment, I'm upset with myself because my dad sees my mistake, not his daughter.

Well, now I'm feeling the pressure of it all, but really the world war two is just getting started; We have to inform my boyfriend's parents.

When my boyfriend told his mom the news, she fainted. Can you imagine? I knew she was devastated. She was worried about her son's future. Thankfully she landed on the bed. (boy! if emojis were out then she would have gone viral!) His father wasn't happy either but took the initiative to come over and went to the doctor with me and my mom and my boyfriend to confirm the pregnancy. I believe that's when both of our parents actually became friends. After the doctor confirmed the pregnancy my mom called our former pastor who was a friend of the family. I wasn't sure what the real intent to invite the pastor over to the home was all about at the time. I wasn't sure who needed Jesus more, myself or **my** parents. But we definitely needed someone who could pray.

The pastor came over to talk with us. It wasn't funny then, but it's definitely funny now; my sister came home from work and saw everyone at the house talking including the pastor. You could cut the tension with a knife. So my sister poked her head in the room and said, "I guess your not fixing dinner, tonight mom"? I will never forget that. She had no idea what was going on. After talking with everyone and weighing all my options, I decided to have an abortion. It was a tough decision to make.

The U-Turn

It's the day I was supposed to have the abortion, my mom and my child's father were with me, and we went to lunch before going to the doctor's office where I had my appointment. I was so confused. My emotions were everywhere. I was scared, feeling alone but yet surrounded by those that loved me. I was in a complete inner turmoil because I didn't know what to do. Do I make the decision that is best for everyone else involved or, do I make the decision in fear and keep my baby because that is what I really wanted to do. However, I wanted my mom to decide for me, but she wouldn't. Isn't it amazing how in life we have the ability to make sound clear choices when it's something we want to do? But when it's at the cost of others we look for a way of escape. Never permit yourself to run from your life's greatest lessons. Because these situations are life lessons and will reveal your maturation level and where you are mentally. But quite often when we are faced with fear, fear will expose us to the present moment and not the faith to see it through. I thought that maybe If she made the decision she would be happy with me again. I had to make a selfish decision. I had to make a decision that I was not sure would be a popular one for all parties. But it was the decision that my soul was screaming out to me inwardly, and it was louder than any of the fears that were competing with the shame I was enduring. Now and then you have to make decisions like that. When people make decisions for other people it will always be an inner struggle because you didn't make the decision by yourself. My child's father asked me not to go. He told me we were going to be together and we would be ok if we had the baby. I was so relieved because I didn't want to have an abortion. My mom was also relieved I didn't go through with the abortion, but she let me make my own decision. I remember, I had on a shirt that day that said the earth is made up of flowers and other living things. My mom later told me she knew that was a sign that I should not go through with having the abortion. To this day she still has that t-shirt. So we canceled the appointment and went home to figure things out. Unfountenaly, His parents were not happy with the new decision I made not to have the abortion. They didn't think we were ready to be parents and said they would not support us at all. They also said that they were going to put my child's father out of the house. His father told me I would be a horrible mother; this had turned into a real-life nightmare, and it was not in a movie, but it was the reality show that was not a script. It was my life, and I had the leading role! Part of me thought that maybe his dad was right. I knew I was young and still living at home, besides I knew nothing about being a mother, I was still being taken care of myself by my parents, and one of the major truths was I also knew I needed to finish school. Fortunately I didn't listen to the opinion or unkind words from my boyfriend's father. I didn't buy into his belief of what he thought about me at that time. What I realize is what a person thinks of you is not necessarily what you will become. How they see you or even judged your mistakes is not your concern. Because we all make mistakes and we all feel as if we've not only let others down but there will be times or seasons in your life when you will feel you have failed yourself. But when those moments happen, you have to make a u-turn and reroute your way Of thinking and get back on the path called " GET UP." The road called " GET UP" will always be met at the intersection called " Another Chance".

Even though I was dealing with so much, my mother made me tell my family I was pregnant. Most of my family were disappointed in me. I was told I was setting a horrible example for my younger cousins. However, I had a rock in my corner. My grandmother was actually relieved when I told her I was pregnant because she thought I was really sick. On the other hand, My sister told me she loved me and that she and her boyfriend at the time, now her husband would raise the baby for me. My brother was also supportive. I think he was happy it wasn't him. As I think about just the fact that they loved me enough to step in, I realized sometimes love, and support are all you need. I knew I had messed up, but the turning point happened when I felt loved by the ones that could see my mess but were willing to give me a miracle. Yes, I said a miracle, because miracles happen unexpectedly.They will always outlive the mess up.

Can the Church say AMEN

At church, I felt like I was such an embarrassment to my family. I was in the choir and an usher, so people were shocked that sweet little Karen was pregnant. The looks and the whispering were awful, but it was the comments said directly to me that were even worse. Lots of people judged me and had not such nice things to say. At the time, I didn't realize the saints and the "aint's" all worshipped together in church. But you could only recognize and identify who was who when it wasn't them that was caught. The saints show love because they understand grace, but then "aint's," well, you know who they are. They will always handle the broken as if they have forgotten how many times God has forgiven them. So my advice, don't focus on the ones throwing the stones, focus on the one that says, "you without sin, cast the first stone."

But at that age, I felt like everyone was turning their nose up at me, which made me feel so bad for my parents. Not only did I feel judged by my church family, I felt judged at school too. Boy! When it rains, it pours. I will never forget while walking down the hallways I heard all the things people said about me. Actually some of the same stuff I used to say about girls who got pregnant in high school. That certainly taught me not to ever judge a person or a situation that you have never been in, what a lesson lived.

There's a Thin Line Between Rejection and Protection

My father drove me to the bus stop every morning, so I wouldn't have to walk. So as you can see, my father had a turning point with how he felt about my pregnancy. The man I have known all my life was now the protection and not the rejection. When I got too big to walk around school and carry my books I started homeschooling. I was glad that was even an option. It made my last few weeks of being pregnant a lot easier.

It's was a blessing in so many ways. My father, whom I knew loved me, was now seeing me as his daughter again and not the mistake I had made. Things were beginning to get better. I had Jordan on the 19th of March on her father's birthday. By this time I was 17, and her dad was 18. There were so many people at the hospital. I'm pretty sure there were over 20 people there! I could hear the loud cheer from my room when they announced it was a girl. Everyone was so excited!

After having the baby, I did homeschooling again. I went back to school when Jordan was two months old. We lived with my mom and dad. My Sister kept Jordan every day until I got home from school. Even though I had a lot of help from both of our families I was always responsible and put Jordan first. I also made sure I kept up with all of my schoolwork. I ended up still graduating on time at the top of my class with a 3.8 overall GPA and Jordan was at my graduation.

I even went to college for a little while to study radiology.

The Reality Of TURNS

You too may have to face challenges in life, but don't ever lose confidence in yourself. I had to hold my head up and keep going no matter what people thought. More often than not the main people who are judging you have been in similar or worse situations but never got caught or made a different decision.

Even when you think a situation you are in will never get better, it can turn around at any moment. I was so happy because I felt like everything was moving in a positive direction. And it certainly didn't take long for Jordan to steal the hearts of everyone.

The CROSSROADS

Just when it seems like there's a glimmer of light in a dark season, sometimes things seem to go dark again. My singing group decided if I had a baby, I couldn't be in the group anymore.

I was devastated because of the group, and being a singer was my dream. In addition to that, the relationship between my daughter's father and I started to decline slowly, but surely we began to grow apart. Having a baby at such a young age was not only tough, but it was hard on a young relationship as well. Now that he was in College he decided he wanted to date other people. I was heartbroken, and I was angry. Instead of just leaving me, he cheated on me. It was awful. I was heartbroken because I wanted my family to be together. I was angry because I thought we were best friends and he would never do that to me. I really thought we would be together forever. It was all so stressful. I remember all the stress I was dealing with was caused by wanting this moment to be something it was not. When I prayed and accepted this season for what it had to show me, it allowed me to see hope in a place of despair.

Shortly after that, my manager from my singing group called me one day and asked me to come back to the group. Of course I said yes. I went back to the group and was so happy. I couldn't believe I had another shot to pursue my dream! I was nervous to see the girls again because I knew they were upset with me for deciding to keep the baby. However, I was pleasantly surprised when I was greeted with open arms. They had really missed me when I left the group. I dropped out of college, and I moved to NY with the group. I left Jordan with her father. I will never forget one day he called me, and all I could hear was Jordan crying in the background. My heart sank. I panicked. It was the worst feeling in the world to hear my child crying, and I couldn't be there or do anything about it. She had fallen off her bike and gotten really hurt. That was another turning point for me because I knew I needed to be home with my daughter. Even though I really enjoyed my time with the girls, following my passion, and all the things I was able to do with my singing group, I needed to go home and be a mother. The group decided to end, and we went our seperate ways. They are still some of my best friends today, and along with my sister Traci one of the members of my group Sharon are godmothers to my daughter Jordan. She also has some great men in her life besides her father.

Her Godfathers are my brother in love, Darnell, her father's brother, and her father's best friend.

"HER" She Never Quits

I decided to come back home to raise my daughter. I got a job singing at funerals. As a matter of fact, I worked for three different funeral homes. I am sure I have sung at over 1000 funerals; however, I realized this was a short-lived career because my audience was always dead…no applause or standing ovations from them. Hahaha! Sorry, I couldn't help myself.

But I knew I needed a job to provide for my daughter, so what better way to do that than doing what I love. Singing was my joy, but the reality was I was singing in hopes of bringing comfort to families in one of the most devastating times in their lives. That was really tough.

I also worked at a mental health facility as an HR Rep. the money was actually good, but I had no time for Jordan. I worked six days a week, some days from 9 am to 8 pm. My next turning point was the day I forgot to pick my daughter up from school because I was working so hard. That's when I started working my LegalShield business and was able to leave corporate America at the age of 32 and work from home for the last 11 years. Never Underestimate "the you" that you've never met. The strength, the fight, the confidence within oneself sometimes can only rise when there is a need for them to stand up.

Being a stay at home mom made all the difference in the world with Jordan.

We are best friends because we grew up together. Both sets of Jordan's grandparents are also the best of friends because, Jordan brought our families together, and I have a great relationship with her father's family as well. They now tell me all the time how good of a mom I turned out to be. Still to this day Jordan is their only grandchild! My parents were also extremely happy about their granddaughter. In fact, my mom and dad have gone above and beyond to be at every celebratory milestone, birthday party, and sporting event for Jordan—her two grandfathers being the loudest and most proud at every event!

Still a single mom now, but my daughter's father and I co-parent very well and have a great friendship. It's been hard but worth it.

Jordan is the best thing in my life, and I'm super proud of her! She graduated from Towson University with a Bachelor's Degree in

Elementary Education. She's a fantastic kindergarten teacher, and her students absolutely love her! Because I've been blessed to run a home-based business that generates a nice 6-figure income and provides time leverage, I get to volunteer in her classroom frequently.

Despite being labeled by society as a statistic, despite the fear, despite feeling like a disappointment, despite having my heart broken, despite the naysayers, everything turned out great! I own a beautiful home, I travel the world, and more importantly, I have a story that inspires others who may feel like their current circumstances define their identity or determine their future!

I always wonder where I would be or what God saved me from by blessing me with Jordan. She is the best thing that has ever happened to me.

I didn't do it the way society says you should, but I did what was right for me, and it turned out that it was right for me indeed. I wouldn't change a thing about my story.

If I can leave you with a few things that I learned during my journey they would be:

- Your current situation is not your final destination.

- Don't be around people that tolerate you; be around people that celebrate you.

- Never let the way others feel about you change the way you feel about yourself

- Never dumb yourself down to be around anyone. Know your worth, and you will attract those who value you.

- Let go of everything that's keeping you from loving yourself

- Your current problems keep you grounded, give you a different perspective, and keep you humble.

- A good church family and daily prayer will keep you focused on who God has called you to be instead of who others may want you to be.

You were given your journey because you are strong enough to handle it.

Dedicated to my brother Robert Lawrence Beverly whom I will always love.

CHAPTER 5

DEIDRA HOLLOWAY

THE SILENT BREAKER

Therefore, if any man is in Christ, he is a new creature. Old things are passed away, behold, all things have become new. 2Corintians 5:17 How did I get here Lord? How did my life end up like this? I never wanted to be like this, and why did you let this happen to me, Jesus? I thought we were cool, and you said you'd look out for me and not allow anything else to hurt me. You promised. I asked you that day not to let that dream or allow my nightmare to come true. You knew I wanted my kids, my husband, my family, so why have you allowed me to walk this path and for so long? Why didn't you stop him from touching me and especially in your church? I was just a kid, and you knew I love you. Nevertheless Lord, DO NOT LET MY LIFE DOWN HERE BE IN VAIN. DELIVER ME JESUS. PLEASE. How I used to love to sing in the youth choir. The hot feeling that I knew Jesus would get all over me, and sometimes I'd pass out. Other times while singing, the warm feeling that I knew Jesus would make me cry and cry. Sometimes the warm feeling that I knew Jesus would make me shake all over. Oh, but how I loved to sing to The Lord. Singing

62

unto the Lord meant the world to me, and the Maestro at our church knew that. This world-renowned and well respected Minister of Music would later turn out to be the predator pedophile that changed a young girls' life and love for music, the church, and gospel forever. We were at rehearsals one Saturday, and he asked a few of us to meet him upstairs to go over a couple of songs. Something felt strange as we climbed the long flight up the steps. I turned to one of the girls, who happens to be my good friend, and I asked her, "do you feel funny like something is not quite right?"

She responded, "a little bit, but there are four of us."

The special rehersals went great, and all fears were gone. Later on, another special rehersals was called, it went okay, but this time it wasn't the four of us, just three. Soon the special rehersals up the long flight of stairs became the two of us, my friend and I. I couldn't quite shake the odd feeling, but my friend didn't seem bothered. He asked my friend to get something for him, which left us alone. Before I could run down the stairs behind her, he grabbed me and began to touch me, groping and trying to kiss me. All the while saying, don't tell anyone, and it won't hurt. I was trapped, lured with the deception of the Maestro and all the while, everyone thought he was the greatest. Suddenly my friend came running back up the stairs. She saw the look on my face and said, let's go, Dee. We left, and I never made another solo rehersals up those stairs.

From that day forward, I fought between my love for singing in church and the disappointment of what goes on in the church. How can I still participate and not get close to the pedophile? How do I protect my family's reputation, and how can I not become an embarrassment to my Father? Isn't that how the devil does? Put all the pressure on the kid. I wasn't concerned with protecting the Maestro, but I absolutely could not lose my Daddy. The silence begins; time would pass, and I honestly don't remember how long we bobbed and weaved through it all. There is nothing like a childhood friend that the bond is eternal, and indeed without my girl, I never would have made it. The Maestro never stopped his trying, and we kept avoiding him until that day. The bus pulled off without about four or five of us, and we had to ride with him. I'll never forget that big white Buick with the red interior. Things were cool at first, kids cracking jokes and laughing up a storm. Suddenly, he remembered that he'd forgotten something at home and needed to pass by his house. He started by dropping two of the kids off because we were near their homes. My friend and I stayed farther away, and he continued as if he was taking us home as well. Then he asked if we would mind riding to his house so that he could get what he needed.

Somehow, my friend's sister ended up coming to his house and picked her up. I'm left all alone with the one person I've managed to avoid being alone with for quite some time. He went to the bathroom and said that we would leave as soon as he comes out. All I could think was, my friend was right, this would be over soon, and I'd be home in a jiffy. He took so long in the bathroom, or maybe it just seemed that way. The door opens, and I'm relieved. Finally, let's go. As I am walking towards the door, he grabs me from behind and tries to kiss me. I pulled away, saying all I want to do is to get home. What kind of man of God is this? What kind of preacher goes around trying to do things like this and especially a married one? What's wrong with this man? This is what kept rolling around in my head, and how can I get out of here? He came at me again, and I fought with him, he threw me on the sofa and being a heavy man, I couldn't get him off of me. It seemed like time stood still for an instant or something like that and internally, a different young lady emerged. From that day forward I didn't talk the same. My laugh was different. I fought more in school, and anger became my friend. Later that evening, my friend called to check on me, and the first thing she said was that she couldn't stop worrying about me. This time I didn't open up to her. I couldn't release the words, and I couldn't cry. Life returned to its normal routine, but everything was different. The old folks said it best: IF IT HAD NOT BEEN FOR JESUS WHO WAS ON MY SIDE, WHERE WOULD I BE?

Thoughts of suicide began. Still, I sang. Guess you could say the worshipper in me was being born. Instead of hiding from the predator, I decided to become determined in his face and fight back, the only way I knew. Every rehearsal I'm there, every engagement, I'm there. I didn't want any solo parts anymore, but I will sing and perfect my parts. I could hear music in the air and melodies when I walked down the street. Sometimes the part that the Maestro put together, I could hear them before he ever gave them out. Whatever this is, I thought, I like it because I saw that it bothered him. Sometimes when things got hard, and the voice would tell me to take my life, I'd hear Jesus say. "KEEP SINGING."

The years passed by quickly, but I remember them like yesterday. Twelve years young, fighting and resisting the spirit of suicide that had been released in my life, winning but growing weary. This fight had been going on for several years now. One night my parents were out in the back yard, and the battle became real. Suicide was telling me to go ahead and end this. It was pushing hard and giving me suggestions. It said, go ahead and take your daddy's gun and shoot yourself. I knew where my Dad's gun was, so I walked and looked at it. We were raised around firearms, and I knew how to handle them and how to hunt. The suicide spirit showed me the picture of taking the handgun and putting it to my head. I thought, nope, that's going to hurt. Next, it said, well take the 12 gauge shotgun and put the butt against your dresser and the barrel under your chin, then push the trigger. It also showed me that picture just as if a movie was being played out.

I thought, no, that would be too loud, and it would kill my mother to see that scene. Its final attempt was saying, Go into your mother's room and take her medicine. Her valiums are on the table, and she's outside. You can take the pills, tell them goodnight, and never wake up, and this will end it all. I got up from my room again and went into my parent's bedroom, looked at the pills, and said with a long sigh, yeah that's what I'll do. I'll take mama's pills and go to sleep. This life hurts too much already. I went back into my room and sat on the bed, finalizing the plan. Suddenly, I saw Jesus in full form walk into my room and sat on the bed beside me.

He said, "Dee-Dee, you know how much you love presents?"

I answered, "yes, Lord."

He says, "Your life is a gift from me, and it would hurt me too badly if you gave it back."

I asked, "Is my life a gift from you, Lord?"

He answers, "YES." I hadn't cried in years, but the tears began to flow, and I told the Lord that I wasn't going to hurt him and thanked Him for my life. Suicide had been defeated that night for a 12-year-old girl. I knew that Jesus loved me for real, and nothing could change that at all. The years passed, and now I'm 16, and like any other teenager, life is good with a twist. LOL! But the Maestro and Suicide weren't finished yet. Evaluations. Choir evaluations. Mandatory rehearsal for choir evaluations. I do not and cannot be in a room alone ever again with this man. Yep, everyone else loves him and thinks he's so great, but I know the truth. My friend, the same friend that I'd confided in and helped me stay clear off him was asking how and what we were going to do. I was afraid, but I played it off to keep her calm. TJ, you are forever etched in my heart as a real childhood friend. The day arrived, rehearsal began. Let us pray, lets warm up. We sang like forever. I remember my cousin lost his voice during the rehearsal. The director was worn out, and everybody was tired. It seemed there would be no evaluations this day. The director went to ask the Maestro, and we were all hoping to leave. He came back saying the evaluations were still on, and suddenly something came over me. I heard the plan. When you go in, sit far away, listen, and don't sit at the desk. That's exactly what I did. They called my name, and I sat far away and not at his desk. He begins and goes through the evaluation. He notes the improvements and asks why I won't lead any songs for him anymore, but he already knows the answer. All I want is to get out of there. My friend had gone before me, and she told me how it went with her. It went exactly as she said but with one exception. He finishes and says, that'll be all, and I get up to leave. He drops a pencil on the desk, and it rolls onto the floor. I still hear the words playing in slow motion.

"Will you get that for me, please?" He said. The pencil falls to the floor, and I had to pick it up. He swirls his chair from around the desk and grabs me behind my head. Pants already unzipped and an erection, he tries to force my head down to his penis. I couldn't get away but wasn't going down, and then he ejaculates all over my face. He laughs that satanic laugh as I broke free and ran out of the office. I ran downstairs to the restroom, cleaned myself up. No one came looking for me, and by then, it was night. We had been there for hours that evening. I made my way upstairs to the main sanctuary. I opened the side door, and the only light was from the hallway where I was. I went into the dark, felt my way to the altar, the place where we were taught, at the foot of the cross. There in the dark I talked to Jesus saying, Lord, I love you, you know that I

68

do, but I won't be back to this place. That was the last time I went to church, and the last time I sang a gospel tune. Even when I tried to sing, nothing would come out. I could sing all the secular songs and hit the notes, but nothing would come out if it were a gospel song. It was as if the sound of God's word in the song had been shut up and cut off. The Maestro had finished his work. Over the years, there were many battles to fight. I was more than a conqueror in Christ Jesus. Victory is Ours. Troubles come but don't always last, and He won't put more on us than we can bear. It has been a long walk and a longer run, but the race is not given to the swift nor the strong but to the one that endures till the end. Survivors, Warriors, Winners, Overcomers, That's what we are.

What would provoke an established man with profound respect all over the globe to go to such lengths to hurt a child and seek to break a young woman? What profit was there to silence my voice? I'd often ask the Lord, who am I that the enemy took such time to do this when I was so young. For seventeen years, I lived to the left. Still, I could hear the Lord's voice and feel His presence, but I refused to go back into the buildings we call the church. At 33 I was born again, and that's a whole other story of deliverance. Through the process, the Lord gave me my voice back to sing for Him again. Worship leaders, please treasure your gift and keep it pure. I have 15 copyrighted songs given to me by the Lord in early morning prayer that someday the world will hear. Even now I hear Him saying, "many are the afflictions of the righteous, but I the Lord delivers you from them all." Be encouraged and know that no matter what came to destroy you, it couldn't win. God has His

69

hand on me and you, even when it doesn't feel like it, He does. Suicide didn't beat me. Sickness couldn't defeat me. Molestation couldn't waver me. Rape didn't kill me. Abuse wouldn't take me. I AM AN OVERCOMER BY THE WORDS OF MY TESTIMONY AND BY THE BLOOD OF THE SAVIOR. Believe That. In silence, you may suffer from people all around you, but there is one that hears you loud and clear. ***Forgiveness is the*** KEY.

CHAPTER 6

VALERIE SMITH

SORRY, I DIDN'T DIE.

"You won't know how strong you are until you face your weaknesses." Listen. That is the story of my life and the story behind the Glory for me and so many others. Hear me loud and clear. YOU MUST FACE YOUR WEAKNESSES. That is the best way to find out just how strong you are. Here's a loaded question for you today. Are you ready? Are you sure? Are you positive? Brace yourself for this one. Here's the question of the day. How does one courageously keep going when you have no strength? Now, that's a question that needs answers. Well, here's my answer to you. There is no set outline for you to follow. There is no magical formula that works the same way for everyone. Iyanla is not coming through these pages to fix your life. However, I am here to tell you a simple method that has worked for me. Believe that you can, then, do it. Now, I know some of you reading this are like, wait! What? That sounds so cliché. That's so much easier said than done. Am I being punked? No, you are not. That is my truth. Let's start with a few facts about me.

71

I married December 18, 1999, at the tender age of 20. I had not gotten through my Sophomore year in college by then. We had two boys by the time I was aged 21 (January 7, 2001) and 23 (October 5, 2003). We both served in ministry roles in the church as Ministers of Music and a Minister/Prophet of the Gospel. He worked for his family's business, which was cool for him, and it came with perks, which allowed us to live comfortably. We both came from very strict holiness-based roots, and our parents on both sides were still together. Stay with me because that part was important. We pretty much did not come from a "broken home" situation on either side. We worked hard, created a very nice life for ourselves. He was an old soul. Some would call it a caveman when it came to gender roles and how he wanted our household to run. He was the primary breadwinner and mainly wanted me to be his house wife and mother of his children. He was the type that liked to travel a lot and was pretty "churchy" most of the time. Our spiritual covering during the first couple of years of our marriage had us so deep.

Lawd! Some years later, I went back to the workforce, but it was never a permanent thing. So he brought home the money, and I stretched out what we had and took care of our bills, food, etc. I was the wife that cooked often, kept a clean house, and when he was ready for babies, I gave them to him. I was his church girl, his ministry partner, and biggest cheerleader. He was my best friend and first love. What we had was real, and anyone around us knew it. So, guess what? All eyes were on us. We inspired other young couples to marry and live for Jesus. We were that model couple for our generation, and then October of 2005, the ink dried on our divorce papers.

Wow. I know. You weren't ready for that, but it happened. I was 25 years old with a very public divorce. When I say public divorce, I mean everyone around us, including our friends, family, the church folks, and yeah, did I mention the church folks? Yeah, they all knew and had various stories and opinions about "what happened." Some were true. Some were not. Some were partially true. To make a long story short, I was the villain. I was a bad girl. It's not my job to tell you what he did wrong, but I don't mind sharing my wrong. I have always been a brutally honest person. It's not popular to confess certain things, but it freed me. I admitted to infidelity during a very troubled and vulnerable time in our marriage. We separated with the intent to work through it, but it didn't happen. We trusted the wrong leaders with our secrets. Those that we trusted to hear us and lead us were immature. The intent was never to mend us or keep us together but definitely to cosign the divide.

What was unfair and still feels unfair at times was this: I was not allowed to defend myself or share any side of my story for years. God showed me then that if I hold my peace and let him speak for me, I would get to OUTLIVE IT before the eyes of the spectators of my life. God showed me a view of what life on the other side of this embarrassment would be. God even showed me that the preacher at the time that encouraged the divorce and turned a cold shoulder to me during our process would reap a harvest from the seeds he'd sown. Trust me. The manifestation is real.

I will never glory in anybody's demise, but I have acknowledged the fact that reaping is a real thing. Remember that. Reaping is a real thing, and you will know why I said that. Shortly, the contingency that God gave me was hard but worth it. I could not defend myself. I could not give a public statement. I could not respond to the whispers that went on and on even to present day (14 years later) Can you imagine? I was so young and felt so doomed. How was I going to raise these boys without their father in our home? How would I handle him moving on and starting a family with someone else? Would my children fall by the wayside? Were the church people going to cheer for him then slander me? How would this affect my ministry? Would I recover from this? How would this affect the platform that I had in music and with young women? I had not finished college. I did not have a real job other than playing the keyboard here and there or singing with compensation here and there.

On top of that, I had a four-year-old and a two-year-old that depended on me to survive this blow. Lastly, my love for him and desire to be married one time only to the father of my children was out the door. I was 25 years old, divorced, with two children, and no real job. Who was going to want me? Benjamin Franklin once said, "Life is an echo. What you send out comes back." Did it come back? Let's fast forward to a couple of years. In 2008 I met the man that seemed like the answer to all my problems. I didn't want to duplicate my ex. I wanted something different. It was time for me to date again. He was very different from my ex-husband. He wasn't traditional at all. He preferred that I work and pursue my dreams. I released my first single, "Your Grace" while with him. He preferred that I go back to school and become all that I thought I wanted to be. I went back to school while with him. He was not a caveman at all. He cooked for me. He took my kids and became a kid when around them. He was a musician. Wow, he could understand my passion for this music thing. He did not come in trying to be an enemy to my ex or his family. He befriended my ex and showed no signs of insecurity. He accepted that I had been married before, even though he had not. He didn't seem to be bothered by it at all as hard as it was to accept that my ex had remarried a woman that I knew from the church we attended, who was a pretty cool associate of mine that I had known since about 8th grade. I chose to work toward keeping my kids' lives as drama-free as possible. I could have been hateful, petty, and continuously caused problems, but I didn't. I was emotionally ready to move on. I remarried on June 20, 2009.

I think that's right. I'm not trying to be funny at all, but truthfully trauma has a way of erasing some memories by storing them in a place called "never to return." Right after marrying my new best friend, I found out I was pregnant with my 3rd child, who was born March 10, 2010. She came about a week and a half early, but she was born exactly nine months after my wedding. Yep! A whole wedding night baby was conceived. Over those nine months, I found out that my perfect, new husband had a secret of his own that he withheld. So, check this out. Our initial plan was that we would not have any more kids because he already had three children, and I had two. That's a big family. I was going to be with my new, little blended family, so I thought. Well, a couple of weeks before our wedding date, he became very adamant about us sharing a child. He wanted me to get pregnant right away. I was hesitant but wanted to try it for our little girl and had promised myself I'd have all of my children by the age of 30. So, I did it. I agreed to do it one last time. Unfortunately, it was the best and worst pregnancy experience of my life. Around two months after conception, my husband admitted via a public note on facebook to me and the rest of the world that he had a baby on the way that wasn't mine. He withheld the fact that his ex-girlfriend was four months pregnant when we got married. I will never forget the day of being five months pregnant and getting a call in the middle of the night that she was having his fourth child (her 2nd child with him). That's another story for another day. I will never forget all of the sympathy calls, the sympathy lunches, the sympathy dinners, the laughs, the humiliation, the friends I lost in the process after learning how bad they talked about me, the fights between him and me, the sleepless nights, the tears, the questions I had for God, the countless moments of feeling stupid, wanting to kill him, and wanting to kill myself. I will never forget when I was admitted just days after giving birth to my daughter, the sudden, life-threatening spike in my blood pressure due to preeclampsia. I will never forget being admitted at the hospital, scared, and left alone at the hospital to fight through it myself. Yeah, he left me up there after being made aware that my condition was life-threatening, and they needed him to assist in keeping me as calm as possible to ensure my blood pressure levels start dropping. My blood pressure was stroke level. Unfortunately, I made him mad because I was panicking and wanted my newborn baby next to me. My mother and sister had to take her away from the hospital because the doctor ordered. She couldn't stay up there with me while I was being treated. I ended up fully recovering after taking blood pressure medication for four months after being discharged. I remember landing a new job and going back to work before my six weeks were up because bills were not being paid. He was only bringing in money from his part-time job at the church, and gigs here and there. Wow! What a change of scenery, right?

I was juggling two jobs, a new baby, my two boys, my husband, the baby momma drama, naysayers, and just so much until I fell into the deepest depression of my life. God, surely this is not my payback. Am I reaping all of these because of a wrong decision in my first marriage? God, do you even like me? These were a small fraction of the questions I wrestled with daily. I remember coming home one day in 2012, and his clothes were gone. He left. Finally, I didn't have to worry about him staying and gone for weeks at a time, sometimes in my car, leaving me without transportation, and having to find someone to watch my baby while I went to work. I didn't have to worry about if another baby would pop up. I was very concerned about now being divorced with three children by ex-husbands, but I bid him farewell and never looked back or regretted it. So, here I was again. Now at the age of 33, the ink dried on my second divorce decree May 2013.I have been a single mother of three for over six years now. The beautiful part of this story is that both exes are very active in my children's lives, so that's not my issue or story. There are some challenges with one more than the other, but I've survived it. I went through a process of detoxing and restoring. I got rid of the old furniture connected to my past. I didn't follow my past on social media. I minded my own business and only concerned myself with the wellbeing of my children when it came to my exes. Yes, I lost some things along the way. I've lost cars, homes, friends, and material things. However, I never lost my hope. I believed I could give my children a beautiful home one day. I believed my career would take off one day in both music and the corporate world. I believed I could sit in a room with my exes and their wives and not feel uncomfortable whether I had a man next to me or not. I believed I could live without bitterness in my heart. I believed I could allow my children to have healthy relationships with their fathers regardless of how I felt about it. I believed my children could be in the best schools, graduate, and go off to college. I believed my children would be gifted and incredibly smart. I believed my kids could feel loved by both parents without their fathers being in our household. I believed I could co-parent. Listen! I believed I could restore my credit. (Inserts praise break) I believed I could hit the billboard charts independently without a label behind me. I believed I could still live for Jesus and spread the gospel everywhere I go. I believed I could still affect the lives of women all over the world, and I believed I could outlive all of the bad and shine a light on the good.

I believed I could go back to school and complete a degree. I believed that I could upset everyone that expected me to quit, give up, and lay down and die. Guess what? Through the grace of God, this chick did it. I have accomplished the very things that I BELIEVED I could. I am not bragging or boasting, but I am saying I faced my weaknesses and became the strongest version of me, and I'm still not done. In the words of my song, dream, "but you still said qualified with dreams aborted and broken vows, you said it's my season now, I can dream." That's what I did. I saw it then believed it. Today, my children are ages 18, 15, and 9. They all are doing very well in school. My oldest son is going to college in the fall. The boys' father and I are friends and have never had any major blowups over the years. We get along better than most exes, and there's never been anything more to it than co-parenting and friendship since divorced. My finances have increased at least three times more than where I started. I am a grinder, and I love what I do. I am a manager for a Class, A Luxury Apartment Community, the Minister of Music at my church home, an Independent Artist that has shared the stage with countless National and International Gospel and Secular Artists, a Professional Vocal Director, and Professional Background Vocalist. I recently performed in two major stage plays as the leading lady featuring Grammy award-winning stars and stars that have performed with Tyler Perry, Sean "Puffy" Combs, and other major platforms. I will be touring in 20 cities with another major stage play and just living my best life. The best part about the tour is that I still get to be home throughout the week and enjoying my children and family. Lastly, I'm now a book author. I've made some mistakes in this life and will never be perfect, but one thing is for sure; God's hand is on my life, and I'm genuinely reaping the harvest God promised me, taking back everything the devil stole from me. The joy of the Lord is my strength.

CHAPTER 7

JASMINE BROWN

MAJORS & MINORS ...THAT IS THE QUESTION

The Age 11 was MAJOR

Psalm 46:55. God is within her, and she will not fall. God will help her at the break of the day. My mother was pregnant at ten and had me at 11. Through the agony of having a teen mom, I wanted to kill myself at 11. The pain and hurt that is discovered through generation after generation is what got my attention, so I started asking my grandmothers questions about their past and history to see if it was by chance that I'm standing in this place that I'm in. I felt all alone in this world as if no one could relate to me the pain I felt. I began with my paternal grandmother; She stated that her mom beat her with pots and pans and always talked down on her. "This all sound too familiar." After I spoke with my maternal grandmother, who co-raised me, and she stated that she was like the black sheep of her family. Her mom was working with less, and her sisters and brothers never seemed to get a grip on a loving environment; she also stated she was raped as a little girl.

81

These all sounds way too familiar. I now understood that I came from a bloodline of a mess, not just from my mom's side but from my dad's side as well. I then wanted to become the solution of this pit-hole I felt deep down inside. But first I needed answers on where I came from to understand what I was dealing with and how deep it was so I could understand my battles.

BEING DIFFERENT

I knew for sure as a kid that I was different because I kept seeing pictures and glimpse of the future. I didn't know what It was, and I kept asking my grandmother who co-raised me what I am like. I had no real understanding of who I was. For sure, I thought about positive things in every bad situation, and for the most part I was a problem solver. I wanted to create solutions behind non-sense. So I began to spend a lot of time with GOD and seeking help for my life and who I was called to be. As I spent more and more time in my bathroom shower with the lights off in a high phase of meditation, God would reveal to me different things. One consistent thing that was revealed to me from the age of 7 in my room is Stone mountain, at my grandmother's house, I was speaking in front of a large crowd. It looks like I was at the moment. I kept envisioning "Public Speaker," and when the vision came, at seven years old, it weighed heavy on my heart. It's like I felt it, and I was operating at my full potential. It was like I was in my place. I felt in my spirit that was who I was already. The thing Is, I was so good at so many things. I had no real focus on my purpose. It was all about right now results and solutions.

MY BLOODLINE

My mother was a hairstylist. I started helping her at the age of eleven. It was like when I saw something I can repeat it with my hands using my vision. If you told me something, I would ask you what you said many times until I can create what you are saying in a vision. (LOL) From watching my mom have clients and seeing her getting paid, right away, it clicked in my head. I work now, and I get paid now (Simple), then if you're good, you get tips, clients love you, they refer more people, and you grow a clientele, which consists of steady money in your hand. Being that my mom was a hairstylist, my dad was a hairstylist/barber, my dad's brother was a hairstylist, and my mom was a hairstylist/multi-business owner. It ran in my bloodline, and it's easy for me to be in the "Beauty Business" or self-employed. My grandmother on my mom's side is a preacher. My aunt is a preacher, cousin is a preacher, granddaddy was a preacher, and father is a deacon. Ministry runs in the bloodline of my mom's side of the family. On my mom's dad's side of the family, they can hustle you out of a pin. What I love about them is they are transparent about who they are. I'm just a gumbo pot. My purpose is something I ran into. I didn't want the heavy responsibility. But I knew I had to go back and save "HER." But it wasn't simple. Yes, with GOD It went a little something like this. Yes, God was on my side when I get around to it or when I feel like doing it. God, who am I to speak in front of people? My license is suspended. I stay in a one-bedroom apartment. I had a stillborn when I was eight months pregnant, and then I lost my oldest son in a court battle. Right after that, two car accidents and before all of this, I was a stripper trying to survive. My husband and I just split up and on the verge of a divorce.

I cried out to God, "are you sure you want me because my track record isn't perfect. I'm not sure if I would be a good representer for you and your kingdom."

God gave me a straightforward answer, "I still want you."

Then I kept seeing visions about me being on Tv. I went to God. "Now Lord, I'm from summer hill, all my folks talk slang, and I've been trying to shake this accent, and its been hard to do so. I can't see myself getting up there sounding crazy." God resounded, "when I chose you, I took all that into consideration. If you can dare to go to the club and get naked in front of strangers, I want you to have that same courage to get on the stage of the kingdom and save lives with realness. The people who are called to you and your ministry will relate and understand you. You're not going just to save random people. You are going to save your self through other people."

"Her" This was something I had to digest, fast, pray over, go into spiritual warfare over, and cut many people off. But it meant no good to me submitting to others and the world and not to God. What is it to gain the world and lose your soul. I took my "STAND WITH BOLDNESS." Understanding I made it out of my car accidents alive, I was riding out on extra credit because I could be dead. I said, God If you want me to talk to Birds, ducks, or kids, I'll do it. I knew I was riding out on Grace, and I had a job to do on this earth before I die. I could not take this lightly; this is my life we are speaking about and the many lives that will come through this ministry, my purpose, my life, and the many lives that will be saved just for real. Yes, to know God is real. Now I'm standing in my purpose. I took many breaks from social media. I delete my apps and come into God's presence so he can be my Leader in this walk. I'm hungry for helping the generation and legacy of our people change and become more effective in their daily walk with God.

LABOR AND DELIVERY

Being amongst God's people is like a labor and delivery room. It's like you're the nurse, and God Is the Doctor. You're not physically doing all of the work when you let God operate totally in your life, you are the assistant/nurse, and he comes in and takes over as the Doctor. There have been times that God would put other people on my mind, and I would have to instantly start praying for them, or he will tell me to do something, and I would have to do it. One thing about this work is that I understand more and more each day. Luke 12:48 But he that knew not and committed things worthy of stripes shall be beaten with few stripes. For unto whomsoever much is given, of him shall much be required, and to whom men have committed much, of him they will ask the more. I started on the book "The Power of FAILURE" then "Her" and all the while, I have committed myself to two projects same timing, back to back. My eyelash extensions training ministry Takes off. Classes back to back non-stop, and then we birth a lashline all in the same

85

timing. Money is coming in, but the cost of what it takes to run a full business and work on several different projects at once is very costly and tiring. But I was speaking with my assistant saying can you believe it. We have been busy non-stop I can barely see my head spin. We laughed, I said I would rather be busy on Gods timing than sitting this one out. Someone is somewhere saying I wish God could use me, and it's their season to sit on the bench and watch the game, which is required to learn the game. I smiled at "Her" "Gods Timing." Being a leader, it will cost you everything. Words from the wise; it would be better to be prepared, and the opportunity doesn't come than not to be prepared when the opportunity comes

"HER"

My words to "Her" Focus on your purpose in life. Keep God first from the pit to the top of the world. You are never too low to call on God and ask for his direction. Your sin is never too much to ask for his forgiveness. Your situation is not too much for him to use "you" for a time such as this. We need all of our soldiers of the body of Christ to get on board and base, poor or rich, dumb or smart. He takes the unqualified and qualifies them I'm a living proof of someone that should be on drugs or worse of a prostitute, but he saved me. God saved me and made away out of no way. He made me not to fit into the world on purpose. He made me an outcast with men of the world so I can be an in-cast with him. Now I don't just hang out or become friends with just anyone. I allow God to qualify the people that will be around me. From

86

assistants to the people I train/teach and the many different projects I agree to handle. Moving with God is walking in power, and now that I've been walking in power. I don't want to move any way but His way. But I had to be willing to submit to his will and be ok when he says something that I disagree with. Also, when he says no, that takes courage because I would rather be in God's will than to be out of his will Dancing with the devil. You must have a made-up ready mindset about your life and your life's purpose. You are breathing for a reason. Spend time with God to find out your why. Submit to his will and put him first. God is a God of order. You must focus on his word so it can operate in your life. Your situation is momentary, your purpose is the place you will reside in and move in. I encourage you to take this thing called life very seriously

CHAPTER 8

TIFFANY PEOPLE

GRATEFUL.THANKFUL.BLESSED.

Before beginning my story about me, I want first to tell you a little more about you. I want you to know that you deserve every good thing that God has prepared for you. Believe me, when I tell you, God has something up His sleeves concerning you. It is no accident that you are reading these words. The Bible says every good and perfect gift comes from above, according to James 1:17. That means God has all kinds of good things in store just for you. Yes, you! Blessings, gifts, and surprises. He has lots of great things planned for your future. I'm talking amazing things you know absolutely nothing about. How awesome is that? Believe it.

LIFE BEGINS

Now I didn't say all of that to say your journey will be easy from now on. That, because you're favored, loved, and blessed, you'll face no challenges. Has your life been a breeze thus far? I'm sure your answer is not yes. I wish I could say I have lived my best life, that life has been nothing but grand to me. But that would be the farthest from the truth.

And as you already know through your personal experiences, life comes with many highs and lows. Ups downs, mountains, and valleys. Some things life throws at us will and does catch us off guard, but some are the result of the decisions and choices we've made. But one thing I truly love about God, that no matter the circumstances, He promises never to leave us nor forsake us! Deuteronomy 31:6 speaks on this truth. The promises, plans, and the word of God concerning your life are sure. Amen! So ready or not, you have a great future coming. So with that being said, I will now tell you a little about me.

PUZZEL PIECES

God has brought me a mighty long way as they say lol! The things I have seen, the places I have been, His grace, love, and mercy is nothing short of amazing. Growing up was not easy. I was raised by my step-grandmother and grandfather in a three-bedroom and one bathhouse. I lived there also with an older brother, older sister and a step-aunt. My step-aunt was in a wheelchair and shared a room with my sister and me, and we both cared for her. My mother and father were both rolling stones. Their lifestyle and drug use keep them from raising their children. My Mom has nine kids, and my Dad has six. They only had three together; my older sister, older brother and me. From my earliest memories growing up I had to learn survival skills very quickly. I remember being around four and a half or five years old and playing outside in the front yard by myself when I ran right in front of an all-black snake. It nearly scared me to death. My first thought was to run into the house and tell my Grandmother. So that's exactly what I did. I ran as fast as I could. My heart was pounding. Surely she would come and rescue me from this snake, I thought. I ran past the kitchen into the living room. There she was sitting in her favorite recliner chair. She was watching her favorite daytime soap operas she loved to watch.

"There's a snake outside in the front yard, "I said.

There was a brief moment of silence, but no answer. She didn't respond nor take her eyes off of the television. I repeated it only this time louder.

"There's a snake outside in the front yard."

At this point, she's very upset and angry that I disturbed her. She turned and yelled at me

"What are you telling me for? Go kill it."

Now, as you may be thinking, who sends a four or five-year-old out to kill a snake by themselves? Well, she did, and at that moment I turned around and walked away. Back outside sadden and seeing that I was on my own, I didn't know what to do. With my Grandfather at work, my brother and sister in school, there was no-one to turn too. So thinking quickly I walked around to the backyard, (where my grandfather kept all of his garden tools) I grabbed his farmers hoe and headed for the front yard. The snake was still there by the time I made it back. Even though I was afraid, I still lifted the garden tool and swung as hard as I could. With one swing I chopped off the head of the snake. One of my first very profound memories at such a young age, talk about courage amid fear. I picked up the body and head of the snake and pushed it down the drain pipes that were on the side of the street. My grandmother and I never spoke about that moment again after that.

THEY ARE ALL PRECIOUS IN HIS SIGHT

Shortly after I began preschool, my birthday was eleven days too late, since your birthday must be before August 31st to start school. So having to sit out of school for a year unable to attend kindergarten my grandmother enrolled me in the head start program. I love going there at the beginning: the teachers, the meals, new friends and recess. Headstart was going great until one day while we were playing outside, a boy came up to me and asked me did I want to playhouse. I said yes. As a little girl, playing house to me meant pretend cooking, pretend cleaning and pretend acting like you just came home from work. Playing house to him who grew up in a different environment meant something different I would find out. He took my hand and said let's go over there, so off we went. Once we were around on the other side of the playground, he got close up on me until he had me pinned against the wall. He lifted my dress and grabbed me hard in my private area, and tried to put his hands inside my underwear! It happened fast, but I pushed him off of me and ran and caught the leg of the teacher. I was terrified. The teacher looked at me like something was wrong with me. It was annoying her I was hanging around as she tried to talk to the other teachers, so she told me to play. I couldn't. I felt like the only way to keep him from doing that again was to stay close to her. I hated every day of head-start after that. He would always look at me every day after that like he was waiting for his opportunity to do it again. It was one of my first creepiest feelings ever. I never wanted to go back but always had to and when I did I would stick underneath the teacher at every recess. I never played on the playground again after that and always followed the teacher. She got so upset by it she told my grandmother I wouldn't listen when she would ask me to play outside l. I got in trouble. I never told anyone about that. You're the first.

THE MERRY-GO-ROUND & ROUND

The next eight years of my life with the school were spent being bullied. I was bullied for several reasons. I was bullied for being too quiet. I was bullied for not having name brand clothes and shoes. I was bullied for the styles of my hair. I was bullied for my glasses. I was even bullied for being raised by my grandparents. As a kid I did a lot of suppressing. I suppressed my feelings and emotions a lot. I stayed to myself a lot. I was being bullied at school and abused and bullied at home. My at-home abuse from my grandmother consisted of brutal beatings, insane punishments, and constant cleaning was her way to keep us in check. She would make us use the same bathwater every night when it was time to wash. I was always the last to shower because we went in order of seniority, oldest to youngest. Can you imagine the color of the water? Black by the time I got in it. We never got to wash ourselves as kids growing. She washed us and would wash us so hard with a scrub brush she literally would scrub the skin off of our bodies. Now my older sister bullied me, and my older brother and she both picked at me because my skin complexion was lighter than theirs. They felt like because of this I was not their biological sister. They would say that I had a different father from them and just picked all the time because of my skin. So I grew up wondering if it was true. Most of all of the abuse at home happened while my grandfather was away. When he was home the house was rather peaceful. I hated when he had to leave for work or any reason. He was my only happy place as a kid growing up. So you can imagine how I felt when they told us that he had a massive heart attack the day before he was supposed to be released from the hospital. You can imagine my world-shattering. I went to sleep with the news he's coming home from the hospital the next morning to he's dead.

LIFE, THE SLIDING BOARD

Losing my grandfather at the age of twelve was life-changing. He had raised me since the age of two. I no longer had my safe place to run. To this day, it still is one of my greatest heartaches. I fell into a deep depression after he passed. I shut down fully. I stopped talking to people. My grandmother tried taking me to a psychologist in hopes of getting a disability check. She thought for sure they would tell her something was mentally wrong with me.

But he told her the opposite. He told her nothing was wrong with me and that I was smarter than the average kid my age. He stated my math level was on a ninth-grade level and at that time I was in the sixth grade. The doctor informed her that I was simply a depressed little girl and that I didn't need to be prescribed any medication. This depression went on until the age of fourteen, when I made my first attempt at suicide.

FROM PAIN TO PUNISHING PLEASURE

I planned to slice my wrist as fast as I could. I remember sitting alone, crying, praying to God that he would allow me to die. As I took a razor to cut myself, the first cut with a fresh razor was deep, and the blood was instant. I froze. For some reason, for the first time in a long time, just that small cut relieved the pain and hurt I was feeling, and the pleasure I felt stemmed from it took the pain away. I didn't attempt to kill myself after that because just seeing the blood helped me in my mind, so I thought. Instead, I became a cutter. I began to cut myself all the time. Any time the stress was too great, or my depression kicked in bad, I would go off to myself and make small slices on my arm, and I would feel better. High-school started not long after I got used to cutting myself, but I was determined to keep that a secret and liven up my life. After all it was high school, and I was ready for a new life! Well, high school, unfortunately, went something like this. By ninth grade my depression had developed into a horrible temper. I became very challenging when it came to authority and teachers. I practically lived in isolation most of my freshman year. It started with not coming straight home from school. I told my grandmother I was studying with my best friend, but when she got tired of covering for me she told my grandmother the truth. My grandmother called the police on me. The next day the police came to my classroom and handcuffed me in front of the whole class and walked me out the door. I didn't know what was going on. They put me in the back of their car and drove me straight to the courthouse, not jail. When I got there my grandmother was already there signing some papers. I was placed in a juvenile detention center for three weeks. When I came home, they placed an ankle monitor on my leg. I couldn't leave the house after 6 pm.

I stopped talking to my crush after he cheated on me, and I started talking to another guy. I would go on to serve five more months in juvenile for breaking my ankle leg monitor rules for hanging out with him after my grandmother gave me full permission. She would later tell the judge she never said that. After my five months in juvenile, I got released. I got back with the ex-boyfriend. Now fifteen and pregnant, I had to attend night school because they felt like regular school was not it for me. One day, I just got up from class and walked out. I didn't say anything to the teacher, I just left. At that time, I felt like I was about to be a mother, so I needed to focus on that, and that's what I did. I had my son at 16. Got married to his father, and by twenty-two had given him three more kids. Nine years total in that marriage, then I left. I'll say we had our marriage problems and I gave up. I couldn't do it anymore

"HER"... I WILL SURVIVE

Twenty four years old now and a single mother of four. When I tell you I did whatever I had to do to take care of them, I did. I provided for them by any means necessary. With the life I lived growing up, nothing bothered me to do when It came to mine. With no mother growing up, I was determined to raise mine and be in their life. I was married two more times after this, and four miscarriages totaled. I was raped twice as an adult. Once by someone, I knew personally. He maltreated me and forced himself on me only to apologize later, and once by a stranger at gunpoint. He was someone I met for the first time in person from online. Honestly, my life has had its ups and downs, but one thing has remained constant, and that's my love for God, but, more importantly, His love for me. When I tried to let go, he wouldn't let me. He always knew even when the fourteen-year-old girl was about to end it all, that I would be here this day, twenty-five years later to tell you that no matter what it is, no matter how big your problem is, nothing and I mean nothing is too hard for God. He sees all. He knows all. He will revenge all for your sake. Trust Him. He has a plan. Amen?

As I end this chapter, I can't help but be GRATEFUL for the life God has given me. I dare not wish or desire to change anything in my life experience. It is because of everything that I experienced, that I am encased in the strength and power that I stand firm in today. I am THANKFUL because God has taught me never to give up. He's taught me to trust in Him always, especially with things I didn't understand. His love and patience was always the constant driving force that drew me in and back to Him. And I'm BLESSED because I get to wake up happy and breathe new life. I get to spend time with my grandbabies and the people that I love. I'm blessed because I get to share my story with a beautiful woman like you! I am genuinely grateful, thankful, and blessed.

Lord and I pray for the lady reading this. I pray for her as she reads these lines that you continue to strengthen her and stretch her beyond her limits. Let her know she is truly loved and covered by you! Lord, in all that you do bless her indeed. I pray that something I said blessed her. I pray this chapter, along with every other chapter that she reads in this book is life-changing for Her.

A special thanks to the visionary for this very anointed project. The beautiful Melissa Williams. She is a Godsent, a general in the spirit, a mentor to me. Just a selfless love. It was her love for God, the authors of this book, and her love for you that made all of these chapters possible. I will end by saying I love you and continue to be blessed by each of these beautiful women in every chapter.

Amen.

CHAPTER 9

DR. NIA GEE

IDENTITY CRISIS

I dentity – the fact of being who or what a person or thing is. *(dictionary.com)* I know for the most part that we know what this definition means and have heard it a time or two, but how often have we used it when it concerns us knowing who we are. As young black girls, we are born into families who don't know the meaning of identity or struggled with who they were as young girls and women that are now grown up and, therefore, never learned to come into their authentic selves thus begetting babies that do the same thing. You may ask why? It is because sometimes we are predisposed to certain lifestyles and normally don't try or attain a change from the environment we were born into. Nobody ever talked about being true to yourself, learning yourself, or even loving yourself as a growing child. So, how would I ever know how to do any of these things as I come into womanhood? Except I fall head over heels in love with a man named Jesus Christ that could change the very essence of who I was and was to become. This would eventually become the story of my life, but I would have to get there first.

Therefore, if any man is in Christ, he is a new creature; old things are passed away; behold, all things have become new (2 Corinthians 5:17 KJV).

GROWING PAINS

"Misunderstood and no one to glean from; as a young girl growing up on the Westside of Chicago and very different, I was misunderstood and had no one to glean from. No one in my family cared enough or wanted to take the time to invest in me, for they would say, "no one did it with them." And no one in my neighborhood that I could identify with or that wanted to hang with me and be a friend long enough to learn what I was going through. Besides, back then, anyone who knows whatever that was going on in your home had better stayed in your home. But little did people know I was angry, depressed, frustrated, unloved, abused (physically, emotionally, sexually, verbally), had very low self-esteem, and honestly wanted to end my life and would later attempt to.

I nor anyone in my circle knew anything about God or Satan for real. We didn't know about generational curses, family spirits or Satan and his tricks/deception that he uses to keep people bound. I was one bound chickadee and had no clue at all. *My people are destroyed for lack of knowledge: (Hosea 4:6).* You see, what should have been some of the happiest times in my life as a child were the worst of times for me. Born to a teenage mother that hid the pregnancy until she could no longer, of a father that wanted to have nothing to do with me and neither did his parents, maternal grandparents that were angry, embarrassed, and just wanted me and this entire situation to go away. Aunts and uncles that felt as though they had to pay for a mistake that was made by their fast tail sister and not them. Being born into this type of situation had already set my life up for a downward spiral of nowhere that would only get worse. The older I got, the less I knew about myself.

Now, thanks to God, which always causeth us to triumph in Christ, and maketh manifest the savor of his knowledge by us in every place (2 Corinthians 2:14 KJV).

You see, with everything that I was given to start life with or what I wasn't given was set to be the finality of my life. She was born, lived a miserable life, and died, the end. How many of you had those stories, or so people thought? Well, we know that the devil is a ball faced liar. Yes, my start was horrible, my growing up looked bleak, and my future was to be nonexistent, but our God had a more excellent plan. Hallelujah!

As I grew up and became a young adult, I am not going to say life was easy for me because, honestly it most definitely wasn't. I had created such a whirlwind-made-up life for myself. I didn't know what was true and what was a lie. Still, as I continued to forge forward and mature in life, I was trapped in the false identity I had given myself, not my God-ordained self. You heard me, the life that I made up for others to believe, including myself (I started to believe exactly what I was saying to about myself). How many of

100

you know that it is a problem all by itself? It's ok to raise your hand because I know for a fact that many of you have created the very same thing concerning your life. Your safety spot, your sweet little made-up life, and that way, you safeguard yourself and the thoughts/words/deeds of people. Well, you can't move forward in ANYTHING, especially the things of God, until you can be honest with the man/woman in the mirror. That Is YOU. When I started not only to see me but be honest with me, I could then conquer with the help of God, that very thing that I had been hiding from; MYSELF! "Seeing me the way God sees me."

Seek ye the Lord while ye may be found, call ye upon him while he is near. (Isaiah 55:6 KJV).

After finding God, it still took many many years before I would find out who I was in Him. My beginnings in Christ were based upon the non-learning, non-committed, non-study on my own of Him. You know the (2 Timothy 2:15) kind of seeking him, Study to show thyself approved unto God, a workman that needeth not to be ashamed, rightly dividing the word of truth. I relied on the pastors that I had to give me what I thought God wanted me to have.

I didn't seek him or his Word for real nor to know Him on my own. Honestly, that's what took my process so long in getting to who God would have me to be. I looked for myself in other older women *(remember I was born to a teenage mother and a family that didn't want me, and besides, they didn't know who they were either)*. I wanted a mother that would help me discover my meaning and love me

101

(because I didn't know what it was like to receive real love either). I looked for it in my husband, getting married at the age of 19, and thought that he (my husband) was going to be my Savior and help me deal with all the issues I had going on inside of me. I looked for it in friends *(I thought they would take away my issues and finally help me walk into being who I was supposed to be. My sister circle).* You know they say you should surround yourself with people that have more than you or are where you aspire to be. Well I did that, and it didn't help with what I was dealing with internally.

There is only, but one that can save a sin-sick soul, and His name is Jesus.

"For God sent his Son into the world to not condemn the world; but that the world through him might be saved." (John 3:17 KJV)

Even though I had gotten saved by word of mouth, I still needed to give my entire heart to Jesus that I might not be condemned, but saved for real by Him, by His Grace. That's exactly where each of us needs to start, giving our whole heart, mind, and committing our spirit to Jesus Christ and allowing Him to be the head of our lives. When I did, those things turned around drastically with how I not only saw myself but how I felt about myself. It was a fresh start for me, and I found my true Identity in myself through God; this is by far the most important step in finding your identity and on the road to recovery from the issues that plagued with it. "I am a New Era preacher."

THE "ENCOUNTER"

After I recommitted my life to Jesus, I was getting dressed one day in front of the standing floor mirror in my bedroom, as I was fixing my shirt in the mirror, I heard the Lord say specifically and audibly to me, "you will be a New Era preacher." A "New Era preacher?" I asked, "what's that?" His response was, "I'll show you." After He said that and nothing immediately changed, I went on to finish dressing and thought no more about it. Mind you that I was going to a mega-church where there was a big-name pastor. I was dressing differently (no $300-$400 rhinestone suits, church lady big hats, matching lap scarves, shimmery pantyhose, J Renee shoes, etc.). I was walking differently, more confident, bold in Christ, not afraid to say and do what I was instructed to by Him. Comfortable in myself and didn't even notice it until one day, I was approached by someone and something that would have normally caused me to stumble. But I was able to handle it with no issues whatsoever, and that's where God began to show me the change that had occurred in me, and how I no longer needed the validation of man, but only needed his validation. He began to show me and walk me through being that New Era preacher He told me about. I started studying the word of God for myself, and seeing that a lot of what I had been taught was just man's way of doing things and not Gods. I wanted to do things His way and His way only, and I wanted anyone that came into contact with me to see that as well. I wanted them to see the Christ in me and to allow them to know that they too could have this. God then began to show me who he had designed me to be in changing my physical appearance. I know this

103

seems minor to you, but it was key in the process of Him showing me who I was to become in and for him. So He started with my hair, at the time I was accustomed to wearing what seems to be the popular hairstyle of the people I was around. The Lord and I say again the Lord had me to go and cut my hair off, dye it platinum blonde, and wear it with spikes all over. At this time, NO preacher was doing this. He then began to change my style of dress and gave me such liberty with what He was doing. It began to free other women at this church that had been bound by man for years. I know they were being liberated because they would come to me week after week and speak these words of liberty directly to me. I would always be courteous and say thank you; however, I knew that this was Gods doing.

This also showed me that my instability in life had been caused by my lack of identity and not knowing who I was. You see, I would follow whoever wherever with whatever they were doing or what the popular vote was. See, when you are in an identity crisis, your thoughts of you are the last ones that count. You don't know you are important, too, and you are important to God. My thoughts were that if I followed and do what the important people did, I also would eventually become important. WOW! What a misconception that the enemy would have us believe, that your only importance is voiced by other people, like you have got to be voted in.

For thus saith the LORD of hosts; "After the glory hath he sent me unto the nations which spoiled you: for he the toucheth you toucheth the apple of His eye." (Zechariah 2:8 KJV).

You are the apple of God's eye. You must position your heart and spirit to believe that, and that only occurs when you have learned to love yourself and the person that God has called and created you to become. "Finding and walking into your true God-given identity."

I know you are asking how I found myself in God, not only how to find myself, how do I love myself that he has created me to be. The answer to that question honestly is that it takes work, but we know God is right here with us through the entire thing.

- You must first do the hard thing in the equation, and that is learning to love everything about you that God has done in you, even the small quirky things that sometimes annoy us, trust that it's a God thing, and someone somewhere may need that very thing.

Oh, did I mention that this is not about you or for you as you find yourself? It's really about the life of the person that you may perhaps one day save. Remember one plant, one water, but God gives the increase. 1 Corinthians 3:7. Our identities are hidden in God, and the more personal time we spend with Him, the more He will reveal to you not only about Him, but He will reveal the hidden things about you as well that makes you an individual.

105

- 2. Value your intimate time with God. Great nuggets of wisdom are dropped during this time. That is key to your identity as you move forward in God.

- NEVER second guess what He has placed on the inside of you that is now coming out to show and challenge the world. You are an individual and therefore, will not look like anyone around you. Embrace the change that you see.

- Let your light shine. Someone somewhere is having a really bad day, and the light of your identity needs to shine forth so that someone can have a little bit of sunshine.

- Comparing is not of God. Please, by all means, don't compare you and your identity to anyone else. It is most definitely okay to admire people, but don't make who they appear to be the finality on what you think is gospel when it comes to yourself. There are so many copy cats out there nowadays that people don't know what it's like to be a unique person any longer. Be authentic, authenticity alone will cause others to gravitate to you because of the false errs they see continually being put on by other people.

- Drown out all opinions of others concerning who you are supposed to be. Only the one that created you Jesus Christ knows who and what your true identity is.

"Before I formed you in the womb, I knew you. Before you were born, I set you apart." (Jeremiah 1:5a,b NIV).

Allow God to mend all of the broken fences in your life and give you a fresh new outlook on who He created you to be. This will be the start of you not only finding your real identity but loving the God-given real identity that you have been entrusted with by our Father.

CHAPTER 10

TAMIKA LAWRENCE

DAMAGED GOODS

The life of the party, the jokester, and the dance machine. She was only the life of the party on the outside, but on the inside, she was dying. When I was a little girl, my family faced a lot of obstacles, none that we couldn't get through, so I thought. In my family as a little girl growing up with a sister and two brothers. We lived in a small house with two bedrooms, a kitchen, and living room. My siblings and I all slept in the same room on bunk beds. My brothers on the top bunk while my sister and I slept on the bottom bunk. Our bedroom was very small, but we had each other, and that made it worthwhile. I remember I hated to sleep in that room.

I would always hear someone calling my name at night. I would get so close to my sister, so whatever it was wouldn't mess with me; I would hear that voice just about every night. I spent the first years of my life until I was about 8 or 9 years in that small home before we moved to a bigger house. I was so excited and happy that we now had a bigger home that my brothers would have their room, and my sister and I would have our room. YES! This house was so much bigger and twice the size of our first home. And fortunately, my family and I were moving right before the next school year when I would be starting middle school. Wow! A new home and a new school. In the mind of a little girl, what could go wrong? We all seemed to be so happy as a family, but that didn't last long.

After a while, I started to notice that there was a little bit more traffic of people than usual coming in and out of our home. It would be all times of night, and for as long as I can remember, it went on for a while. As a child watching all the traffic of people I noticed there were some drugs and alcohol present in my home. Soon after, the home I was so excited to be living in with my family, well, we ended up losing our home that I loved so much. Now, we had to move in with my grandma who stayed literally in our backyard. To get to grandma's house, I would have to walk out the back door and into her yard, and I would be right at grandmas house. Now, our living conditions changed from good to great and from great to jeez. We were all in one room at my grandma's house. Imagine five people in one room, and two of them were your parents. But because time was hard, my sister went to stay with my other grandma. I didn't want to stay there because of the things that happened to me while staying there when I was growing up during the summer.

SUMMERTIME TALES

Staying in my grandmas home was a very hard time for me. I would love to hang out in my uncles' room because his room was like a child's room; he had all the things you would want and beg your parents for as a child. From dolls, toys, coloring books, games, paint you name it. That was his strategy to get you to his room. He would buy all the snacks from my grandma who was known as the candy lady in the neighborhood. He had all these things to offer a gullible child. My uncle would come and get me when everyone was asleep, and sometimes as I would be going out the front door, he would see me and catch me and he will ask, "You want to play a game?" "yes," I would reply. Because as a little girl, I love to play games and have fun. But his playing was different from my playing. The truth is, his game was me being molested. Each time he had me lay on my stomach, and my back was always towards him. Sometimes he would give me a toy or something to play with. I guess he thought that would keep me focused on something else outside every time he had his way with me.

My memory often reflects so vividly. I could remember cringing up so tight, trying not to feel any pain down there. I could still smell him each time I would have to walk past his room. I would try to run so fast past his door, so he wouldn't catch me because that trick didn't work all the time. The crazy part about it is that I still loved my uncle. Sounds crazy, huh? But I wanted him to see how much he was hurting me and damaging me. I wanted him to see the scared and innocent little girl I was beyond the selfish and explicit acts he was doing to me. And as crazy as it may be, somehow in my mind, I wanted him to love me. But sadly, I never felt the love an uncle should have for his Niece.

THE SAFE PLACE

I had this one friend that I played with a lot as a child. We played almost every day. She would come over to my house, and as time went by, I noticed my friend stopped coming around. I would go to play with her, and she could never come out or over to my house again. I don't want to make any assumptions, but I have always thought in the back of my mind and wondering if what happened to me happened to her. As time went on, there was a continuing cycle that almost became the norm. Bills not getting paid and more. Things started to take a turn for the worst, granny started to get sick, and we had no hot water, no heat, or power in the home. It was so bad we had to boil water to wash up. I could remember being in school without any deodorant on, I had not taken my bath in days, and I smelled really bad. I was afraid to raise my hand or talk in school because I could hear the whispers of my classmates. My classmates were making jokes about the musty and sour smell in the room. I sat there trying to act like it wasn't me.

At this point, I'm now trying to think of something to keep me away from that house. We had no money and every place that we had ever lived we had lost due to drugs and alcohol being the top priority. That life destroyed everything we owned. I started to hang out with friends that seem to have good and stable homes. I felt like I needed to be around families like theirs. Their lives and homes were peaceful and pleasant to be around. I was now around positive environments, and that's the life I wanted and longed for so bad. I don't even know if any of my friends knew what was going on in my house. If so, they never asked me or even made a jester to them knowing anything at all. I certainly didn't share anything with them. I was so ashamed and embarrassed to tell anyone what my life was like. I wanted to fit in and be accepted so bad by other people, and the only way I knew how to do that was to do what most of my friends were doing; join the crowd, the who's of the school. So I joined different teams in school to become more like my peers, to occupy my mind and, keep myself busy so I wouldn't have to return home early. At the same time, to fit in with everyone else. In middle school, I joined the gymnastics and track team, in high school I joined the cheerleading squad and along with that came uniforms, camp, camp fees, and let's not forget homecoming dress, prom dress, and graduation camp and gown for graduation. I didn't know that you had to have money to be able to participate in these extra-curricular activities.

How was I supposed to get some money? I asked myself. We had nothing. So, how was I supposed to purchase these items without any money? The only two people in the house that had money were my grandma and my uncle. My parents didn't work, and If they did have jobs, we had no transportation to get around. There were a lot of things that I wanted to participate in at school, anything to keep me away from that house, but I did not have the funds to live the lifestyle most of my friends lived. Trying to be on

112

the same level as them was pretty hard to do when you had no money. In my mind, my only source of getting money was to get it from my uncle. My grandmother took the little money she had to pay the rent and whatever else she could afford to keep a roof over our heads and food in the fridge, so my only other way to get quick money was from my uncle. For him to give me anything, I had to allow him to have his way with me. What was I to do? This is all I knew. Well, I took a deep breath, and in my mind, I knew what I had to do. So, that's what I did.

At this point, I was in survival mode. I don't want to always stay at home. Every chance I got, I took. Yes, I was messed up as a kid to think that my only source of money was to give myself to the man I was trying my best to get away from. I had to have personal items as well, like deodorant, soap, pads, clothes, and shoes. You know things of that nature. I hated myself for having to stoop that low to get money for things I felt my parents should have taken care of. But what were they supposed to do? They had a battle; they were also fighting to survive. I had become angry, bitter, mad, suicidal, very promiscuous. My attitude was horrible. I was depressed, and eventually, all these emotions had taken over.

THE AFTERMATH

I had become fearful of everything except when it came to standing up for my siblings. We were all we had to keep going. The four of us protected and watched out for one another in the midst of what was going on in our lives; it never tore us apart. The four of us grew closer and closer together, and to this very day, our bond is still as tight as it can be. I am so proud to say we all have grown into loving and caring parents, and our lives do not reflect what we went through in our home as children. After having to do things for money, I grew up thinking that if I didn't give myself to whoever I was in a relationship with, that they wouldn't love or care about me. I never knew what love felt like; my uncle wasn't the only man that has ever touched me, groped me, or fondled with me. You know those so-called uncles and friends of the family; they all played a huge roll in damaging my innocence and self-confidence. I hated myself and everything about me; this all happened to me before I was even in high school, and as soon as I thought I had gotten away from it all, there it was again like déjà vu right under the same roof.

I had just graduated from middle school, barely 14 years old, thinking I couldn't wait to turn 18, graduate and leave home for good; those four years couldn't get here quick enough for me. I was old enough to babysit, one more opportunity to escape and get away from hell. That summer, I went to stay with my cousin to help watch after her kids while she worked. One night she had company over, a guy she was dating, he brought two friends with him, the same two friends would come over every time my cousins' boyfriend would come, I don't think he had a car to get there; so, he would get a ride from his friends. They came over quite often, so the kids and I got to know them well, well enough to feel comfortable with them being around. I started noticing that one of the guys would pay attention to me a lot, especially when he was intoxicated or high of marijuana. They never smoked in the apartment; they would always stand outside in front of the door to smoke. My cousin didn't smoke and didn't want it around her kids. Sometimes when they were smoking, we would be outside playing for hours till the sun went down, and if someone was watching us, we were good. This man was my cousins' age, so he had to be in his twenty's, many years older than me.

One night, they all ended up staying the night from being too intoxicated to drive home. There was nowhere to sleep; it was only a 2-bedroom apartment, a kitchen, and a living room area, my cousin slept in one room, and the other bedroom was for her three kids. Whenever I would stay over, I always slept on the sofa, which was where I slept the night they stayed over. He waited until everyone was asleep he woke me up and asked me to come over to where he was lying on the floor, me half-sleep not paying any attention to what was going on, remember I trusted him. I got off the sofa to go and see what he wanted; he pulled me down on the floor, pulled the cover over us so no one could see what was going on, he began to tell me how pretty I was, that he loved me and I would be his little girlfriend. Something didn't feel right, but I was so afraid to get up, he started to touch me and rub his nasty hands all over me. I could smell the marijuana coming from his fingers, he started kissing me, and before I knew it, he was on top of me. It was so painful I wanted to scream. It seemed like it took forever for it to be over, I couldn't push him off me, he was too strong. I was just a girl starting to reach puberty. It happened at least twice that night and each time was horrible. I heard his friend tell him that he was wrong for what he had done to me, but his friend

115

never stopped him. He made sure that I was back on that sofa before everyone got up that next morning. I was as quiet as a mouse the next day and didn't have much to say. I wanted to tell my cousin so bad about what happened, but fearful that she wouldn't believe me.

For the rest of that summer, there wasn't a day that went by that my cousin was working that he didn't come by to have sex with me. "Was this rape?" I asked myself this question. Then, I thought, well you didn't say no, all I knew is that I was too afraid to tell someone, and I couldn't think of anyone that I trusted enough to tell. I never wished for my period to come as much as I did that summer. Screaming silently, I THOUGHT THIS WAS OVER. The summer finally ended I was headed to the 9th grade, destroyed on the inside, damaged, my body was going through all types of changes, my body didn't feel normal.

I started to notice a bad odor coming from down there. I didn't know where it came from or how even to get rid of the smell, nothing. I mean, nothing would make the smell go away. I started to get sick; my stomach begins to ache badly. I felt nauseous all the time, and I couldn't eat anything without it coming back up. I was so afraid that I was pregnant, I had lost so much weight. My mom ended up taking me to the nurse, and she drew what seemed like a lot of blood. I was curled up on the stretcher aching and in so much pain. Mom stayed in the waiting room while I was seeing the doctor; she had no idea what was going on. The nurse came in with the lab results, still afraid that she would tell me I was pregnant, but I wasn't pregnant.

She said, "Your test came back, and you have gonorrhea; would you like for me to tell your mom?"

I said, "do you have to?"

She said, "No, you are old enough to keep this information confidential."

So, mom never knew. What could she do? The damage was already done.

She said, "you know that you can't have kids after having a disease like this, it messes up your reproductive organs."

I didn't even know what gonorrhea was. Everything was happening so fast that night. I didn't have time to process anything, but I heard her when she said I couldn't have kids. What does she mean? Couldn't I have kids? I must have kids. Who else will love me for me? I went numb. After leaving the hospital, mom asked what the doctor said. "Virus." I said, "he told me that it was a virus." It took me almost a month to get better. I was bedridden for weeks. Still couldn't keep anything down, my weight was falling off like leaves in the fall.

I was so ashamed, embarrassed, and felt so guilty that I allowed this to happen to me. I was like damaged goods. I changed into a different person after that. I hated myself, and I hated school. I

117

couldn't function or focus on anything. Being molested and taking advantage of caused me to act out of hurt, disappointment, anger, bitterness, you name it. I felt it. I drew a complete block. My defense mechanism was making people laugh, being the life of the party, anything exciting to hide the hurt and pain I was feeling inside. I was always with a guard up to protect myself and those who I cared about. I grew to have trust issues, needing to be accepted, to be acknowledged, to feel important, I had a strong spirit of rejection that caused me to question if I was worth anything.

The demons that lay and waited on the inside of me took root, waiting to grow and cause destruction. I didn't know who I was or why I did the many things that I did. I never spoke positively about myself. I condemned everything I did. I continuously saw myself as being dirty and unclean, worthless, damaged, and broken.

I've asked myself what I will tell the young girl or lady that's reading this.

1. Having a personal relationship with God played a significant role in my freedom and deliverance. *(Galatians 5:1 NKJV) Stand fast therefore in the liberty by which Christ has made us free, and do not be entangled again with a yoke of bondage.*

2. Being free takes work; you must participate in your freedom and deliverance. God is there to help but, He will not do all the work if you are just sitting back in defeat.

3. Identify where your unhappiness is coming from. If you are not sure, pray and ask God to reveal to you what it is.

4. You must forgive.

    - Forgiveness is not for that person; it's for you. You have to forgive to move forward and be better and able to become what God ordained for you to be. Unforgiveness is never good for anyone. It causes your healing process to be a lie and the wounds to remain opened and fester.

    - Forgive yourself because what happened to you is not your fault. Often we blame ourselves because we feel that we could have done something to prevent that thing from happening, or we could have said something. LISTEN! Whatever happened was going to happen whether you tried to stop it or not; it happened. So forgive yourself and allow God to begin to work on that wound and not let the enemy poke at that continuously would stop its healing process.

1. If the process becomes unbearable, it's good to see a therapist or psychiatrist. Let me go ahead and kill that thought now. Yes, it's okay for Christians to seek help through a therapist or a psychiatrist, I pondered on that same thing for years, and feeling too embarrassed to admit to myself that I need to see someone, because I thought it was offensive to God and it meant that I didn't have faith

that He could heal me, but doctors, therapists, etc. were all given those gifts and put in place so that we could have other avenues for help, this does not mean that you do not believe.

2. Be okay, with not being okay. We have to be honest with ourselves first because healing begins with you.

3. GOD DID NOT DO THIS TO YOU! There's no need to be angry with God for what happened to you. God is not a God that will cause you pain and heartache. He is there to help, comfort, and love you no matter what. The bible says in *Isaiah: 53:4-5 (ESV) Surely he has borne our griefs and carried our sorrows; yet we esteemed him stricken, smitten by God, and afflicted. But he was pierced for our transgressions; he was crushed for our iniquities; upon him was the chastisement that brought us peace, and with his wounds, we are healed.* Jesus came to save us not harm us.

4. Begin to love yourself just as God loves you. Begin to see yourself the way God sees you. After all, EVERYTHING God made was good, and that includes you.

Genesis 1:31a (ESV) And God saw everything that he had made, and behold, it was very good.

5. God can still use you if you allow Him to, we are created new in Jesus, and old things are passed away once we become followers of Jesus Christ.

   2 Corinthians 5:17-18 (ESV) Therefore, if anyone is in Christ, he is a new creation. The old has passed away; behold, the new has come. All this is from God, who through Christ reconciled us to himself and gave us the ministry of reconciliation;

6. Isolating yourself is never the right choice. Being alone while in heartache and pain or bondage gives the enemy room to invade your thoughts and actions. Surrounding yourself with friends and loved ones that will encourage you, pray for you, and love you is a very important part of your healing process.

7. Please allow the tips that were given to be something to use as you begin to be free of the bondage that has been hovering over you for years. I'm not going to lie. This is not an easy process; it takes strength, courage, fight, motivation, and God to make it through this. So put on your boxing gloves and give the enemy hell for the BIGGEST fight of your life.

CHAPTER 11

JESSICA RAPPIT

LET THE MUSIC PLAY

I can still hear gunshots being fired, loud music, the smell of Cush smoke in the air, children screaming, my mother weeping, arguing, and cell doors closing; guards yelling, "lights out." I still remember shattered glass, pools of blood and crying babies. Life as I know it hasn't been easy. I have seen it all. From birthing three children through three separate situations filled with their own stories of despair to almost making it to the big screen. I often ask myself, how did a multi-talented beautiful smart young lady end up here? Since birth, life has been an ongoing struggle. My dad was a professional gambler and a lady's man that found joy in drugs and alcohol. My mother loved him and prayed daily he would change. She later found that being pregnant with his child and consulting with God wasn't enough as he fought and argued with her daily about his unyielding substance addictions. My little body growing inside of her unharmed was my first miracle from God. Since conception, the enemy has had it out for me. I instantly came to see that being carried in the womb of a woman subjected to violence, starts a war everywhere. My mother suffered major health issues, some near-death after my birth and my father suffered the death of his soul through crack addiction. He was the head of our family while his mind was a prisoner of the streets. From rehabs to living with family, my dad never changed, and I witnessed it all. My entire family was like a toxic mafia. From aunts and uncles that schemed, gambled, and finessed people out of their possessions. I believe it was there I was exposed to the gains of a toxic lifestyle. Fair skinned and shapely, I was labeled as "hot" or fast. I got blamed for everything my cousins did. It never bothered me it just changed the way I moved. I became a hustler as a pre-teen, I remember getting whippings for selling the gravel from out of my granny's yard. I told the children that the rocks were magical. I even remember reselling the penny candy that I bought from the neighborhood candy lady turning around selling it for 5cents after she was closed for the day.

As a hustler, I knew better than to fall in love even from an early age. I saw men as competitors or friends, so I used to run with them and fight other boys which often landed me in an alternative school and usually suspended.

THE RHYTHM... I FEEL IT

I was a good student but a troubled young woman. Running and fighting with the boys should've taught me more, as my first unwanted sexual advance came through a woman. My dad met this lady at rehab who had a daughter that was already having sex, and she used to touch me. It was there I was introduced to homosexuality. My family couldn't understand my hate for the girl,

123

never knowing that she was molesting me. With one parent strung out on drugs and another traumatized by our broken existence I grew up too fast, too wise, too soon.

Over the years, I found my drug: creative arts. I creatively distracted myself with God-given gifts staying busy so that I never had to deal with the pain that no one seemed to notice about my broken life. The illusion of busyness made me feel like life was changing for the better. My dreams were indeed an illusion when my mom married my stepfather. He was an excellent provider and never seemed to disrespect my mom, as my father did. My stepfather used to take good care of us, but in return, he felt like if he provided for us, he had a right to sleep with me. He used to sneak in the door of my room at night and masturbate to what he believed was my sleeping body, but I saw it all then. He would get up the next morning and read the bible, so you can imagine the thoughts I was having about God. I can recall one day he picked me up, and the car broke down. While waiting on the tow truck, he asked for a kiss, giving him my cheek as I always did; he grabbed me and kissed me in my mouth. Fear gripped my ability to trust anyone, and that was the moment I began searching for other outlets.

THE SOLO...A CHOIR IS TOO MANY

I began to hang out with a family friend who my sister used to be her hairdresser. I admired her because she was always fly and kept large sums of money and jewelry. She used to call me her baby, and I felt safe with her. She started to let me come to her home after she got out of prison. I never told her why I didn't want to go home. I used to ask her to stay and if she could take me to school. Having no idea, I was running from the molestation at home. Knowing I was trying to escape him, my stepfather would tell my mom to make me come home because "I didn't need to be around her." He only wanted me back to finish the job the enemy had set up for me, so I was forced to go back home. One day I was sick and stayed home from school. He came home early. He approached me and said I'm going to heal you. He exposed his nakedness and climbed on top of me, attempting to penetrate me. I ran out of the door and screamed for my mom. I couldn't take it anymore. To this day the stench of him, the color of his skin, repulse me. Broken and afraid, I finally told my mother what had taken place. She avenged me by shooting a warning shot toward his body. He left, yet somehow later, he returned. The sting of betrayal hit my young heart against my mother. The adult me realized she just couldn't stomach losing again. Yet for a season, she lost me.

I left home, and my life spiraled out from there, I started to rebel and date older men. I formulated this thought in my head that I would never need a man for anything because watching my mom be a good woman seeking love and get abused by my dad and her husband, I hated the thought of letting myself become a victim again. Yet the enemy kept setting traps for me. I was now a pre-teen girl living with a woman in her late 20's learning to hustle, meeting different men, seeing drugs and dating drug dealers, clubbing but still going to school, and I graduated a year early with honors. My toxic journey continued through sexual acts, money and the flashy lifestyle. I was taught by my god-sister how to glorify street life. I'm not blaming her because she was a part of God's plan for my life and tried to help me the best way she knew how.

I continued to live the street life even with scholarships for college for my many talents. I got a full ride to the art institute of Fort Lauderdale, but as lust and love would take its course, I met this guy named Gator, and we began dating. I postponed going to school, never throwing the idea away completely, but I always dreamed of being somebody's everything, and he was getting money. Another path to the fast life. I soon realized that wasn't it. We fell in love, moved in together, took shopping sprees and lived on the night scene, matching outfits, and having the latest everything. I didn't want for nothing. Yet when money got low, he stopped coming home and stayed in the trap for weeks on end. I didn't know he was a drug dealer. He told me he was an investor. He never told me what he invested in. We lived the life that dealers live and it wouldn't be much later that people began to become jealous of him having the beautiful girlfriend, they started to make up lies and telling him about old boyfriends like they were recent, all in an attempt to cause friction and get into his head. Those same friends would run off with his money, send the police after him, which landed me in the middle of situations I had no place in.

SLOW JAMS... THE NEW R&B

I can remember having to quit a job I was working because of the threats of being kidnapped, which eventually happened but God still spared my life and allowed me to escape. I started smoking weed because I was frustrated, in love, and broken. My upbringing led me to believe that this was a part of life. It wasn't until I started getting beaten up by this man that I began to gradually see what I was putting myself through. He took my key so I couldn't leave the house, took my car, I couldn't leave the house with our things not locked up, and if I locked it, I couldn't get back in. I was lonely and began to look for another way to keep my mind from what was happening. I consulted a friend from my past. I tried hiding my horror stories of going with my boyfriend to hotels where he sold drugs and made me lay under the covers with assault guns. He trained me to kill if anybody moved wrong I was always in danger, but I wanted a normal life.

I remember going to his mom's house to talk to her about what was going on, thinking he wouldn't fight me in front of her, but instead he took my head through a wall. I can still smell the sheetrock. I was so embarrassed, she used to get tired of me calling her, and she told me to call the police. Well, every night, I prayed for a way of escape but still praying for him to change. I was torn in between wanting us to work and to have that bad guy turned good relationship, but I was confusing myself and God with my prayers. God made the decision for me.

SINGING AMAZING GRACE

One night on a drug deal gone bad, my boyfriend was set up, and the police busted our home, and he went to jail, they spared me because he pleaded with them that I was pregnant and afraid. Only a few hours later the owners of the apartments evicted us. Instantly, I was pregnant and homeless. I was forced to go back home. When my boyfriend was released, his vengeance was real, and my child and I were real, too, alone; I thought of having an abortion, but my mother pleaded with me not to. I went to sleep that night with her pleadings in my heart. God showed me my future little girl, and I instantly changed my mind.

Starting my doctors' visits would be met with more misfortune. The doctors said they couldn't see my baby in my womb. Week after week the same results. I started to question God. Why show me something I wasn't about to truly have. Again, I turned to drugs. My mind was everywhere, I began smoking while pregnant. I found myself hooking up with my guy friend. I was pregnant, and I was embarrassed to tell anyone. I opened up and told him about everything. I felt safe because he opened his arms to me despite what was going on. Soon after, I began to live with him. I always cried not knowing if that was where we belonged. My life was out of order completely. I continued to live with him. I found out the chances of giving birth to this child were slim and I had to schedule a DNC the following week. I was met with a miracle. The doctor found the baby. However, he found out that her body was severely underdeveloped and stated that she may survive but wouldn't be functional. God had already shown me this baby in my dream, so I had to decide then whether to trust Him or the doctor. I decided to keep my child. I gave birth to a beautiful little girl and moved into a small apartment with my new boyfriend. Trusting his loyalty to me in such a situation we decided to get married. I was still headed in the wrong direction. I often asked myself was I married because I was in love? Or because there was no fighting? Was I married to make people think I didn't fail? Or because I needed an escape? It wasn't until I began selling drugs for my now-husband that I realized I was in a vicious cycle stemming from my traumatic childhood. I was stuck, and not wanting to see my child's father's absence get the best of me, so I stayed. A text message from my husband's college sweetheart asking him if he wanted to see his son, and him advising her to come by his shop while never telling me fumed a sour stench of familiar betrayal. I still stayed.

TRICK OR TREAT.... THE RHYTHM IS GONNA GET CHA

Just as the betrayal was familiar, so was I turning to my talents and artistry to numb the pain. I ran into an old friend, and we began to hang out often. One night, we sat in my driveway super high, and I began to rap over every jay-z's beat talking about our lives and all the pain; this was our new escape. She dated a guy who had a friend that was into music and linked us. We formed a label. It grew to be 50-70 people strong. I was the only female rapper with a lot of game and brainpower. I didn't realize that this, too was about to be another setup. I began popping pills staying in the studio late

129

at night and smoking weed. The fast life, yet again. I brought in loads of cash and attention from men and women. The label was booming, and I was making money doing hair, and recording. I opened for major artists and spit lyrics that a mother should never even know. I was degrading myself and was leading other women to hell. I began shooting reality show pilots, having performances, and walking red carpets with the stars. Arrogance took me, hostage. My husband never said a word. Amid my mess my oldest daughter's father got murdered, I was crushed, but I had to stay strong for my daughter; I somehow muscled up the strength to get up and get back to business. I was about my money and had really lost it after the death of Gator. I began to think of what if I would have stayed I could have spent his last days with him. Regrets, however, the fast life started to catch up with me. I was making money with gangsters, catching the cases, calling the shots and directing women to the bag. I was out of control, and instead of my husband being my hero I felt we began to swap roles. The beginning of our end would be when I got pregnant, and my husband took me to get an abortion. From that point on, we were business partners keeping up an image for our families and social media. I began to step out on him, but I never lied to him, and he never seemed to care which made it worse. I just wanted him to step up, and I was lost, not knowing what I was looking for. At this point, the marriage was open. I think he was more obsessed with people wanting me and the fast-paced life we lived. I stayed out nights then weekends and sometimes months chasing love and money again. I felt I was alone even though I was married, crazy, right? The next series of events would prove that I worked late. One night while leaving the shop I noticed I was being followed. To derail them, I sped through a familiar neighborhood. I called everyone I knew and warned them that I was being followed. No one answered. I drove off the road and cut my lights off. I watched the dudes go in opposite directions, so I headed towards the freeway. Met with surprise, one of the cars dropped off a hill right in front of me. I had almost no way to turn, one hung out the window letting off rounds of shots at me. I was shaking! Reaching for my gun I lost control. As I tried to back off the freeway my Life was flashing before my eyes. I had just told a girl I wore tennis shoes because I didn't know if I would have to run. They never saw me in tennis shoes. I did everything in heels, Not knowing I was prophesying to myself. I jumped out, ran, and hid under the freeway. I knew if they were backing up, they were making sure I was dead, or they were going to finish the job. Distracted by oncoming cars, they fled away. My husband was home with my daughter. He knew what was going on, but he let me live the street life. I guess he was like to hell with it. He wasn't much of a protector. After I was tired, smoking heavily and waiting for the streets to tell me what had taken place, somebody knew something.

I was in my shop's parking lot getting high when I heard the voice of God speak to me. He began to show me images of myself and how he had taken on different forms and bodies to save me. I thought my weed had been laced I began to flip out. It is said when he comes; you had better be ready.

131

Jesus came and met me right in my car. He told me it was time. I instantly began to speak in tongues and texted my now deceased friend Jack. He got my ex-husband, and they took me home, I remember Jack saying, "Sis it's ok, you are fighting a spiritual battle, and that I wasn't crazy I was gifted. That day I gave it all up. I got tired of living the street life and started to go to church. As God began healing me, he did a deep work on my body and image. I was becoming a new woman. I decided to remove sex from the relationship with my husband. He always told me I was his fantasy, but I wanted to be viewed as more than that to him. I stopped clubbing and left the music scene. I decided to focus on my family. The transformation came with warfare as the detox from my former life gave me anxiety and depression. Everyone I used to hang with was going to prison, and God spared me. I felt it was my last chance. As I began to grow in God, it cost me my marriage. I was beginning to heal, and he remained broken. We grew apart. I wish I could say my life was better after that, but salvation is a process. My spirit was saved, but my heart was still lonely. A lonely heart and an incomplete soul ran me into more toxic relationships. In this process I felt God had left me, but really, I kept leaving him looking for a man. I learned how dark of a spiritual walk I was on when I met a man who had been watching me come up on social media. He knew I was full of knowledge I went on a fast often and loved meditation. He knew I was chasing God. Seemingly wise and filled with knowledge of the scriptures, I was drawn to him. Never knowing he would later expose me to vile sexual acts that would include immense perversion and both mental and physical abuse.

He kept trying to impregnate me, and when it wouldn't happen, he inflicted more abuse. I was again a woman on the run.

THE LINE IS THIN BETWEEN LOVE & HATE

Attempting to escape yet another toxic relationship, I ran into another one. Venting to him about my boyfriend, he became my hero. He was handsome and wealthy. His mom passed in the process, and it drew me closer to him and his family. He exposed me to fine dining, pampering, and treated me very well. One day while he was out of town he called and asked me to go get a package for him. He advised that he put some bundles in there for me. I was going to beautify myself and sell some to my clients. I was like "yep bae" bout to help me come up." New business alert! Thinking he was sending me hair from LA, I went to pick up a package from his nephew who was there. I went to the bathroom at the location and was met by the police upon my exit. I had been set up and was now surrounded by cops and agents. I was sent to jail with a $506,000 for trafficking.

THE SHAKE DOWN

It took me sitting in that cell to realize what God was doing. God had to separate me from the world and myself. The woman looking for God in a man found him by herself in the prison walls. I took every day as a blessing. While I was there I wasn't high, and I could hear God's voice again. He ended up using me in that jail to minister to other women with all kinds of trouble and heartache.

I heard him say, "he had to pull me out of the bed with the enemy." This was the way to get my attention, and it did. My bond was made temporarily because an ex held one portion of it, bad decision! However, when I wouldn't agree to go back into the lifestyle, he pulled his piece of property and then next my lawyer got all her money then dropped my case. Landing me back in jail and responsible for the remake of another $506,000. I got to the point where I could do nothing but fight in the spirit. I realized that one way or another, God is going to get you to where he wants you to be. My struggles inspired others as I held on to God. Witnessing my worship and peace through my pain. My scars became pretty. I began to feed more people and evangelize to more people about God. Never revealing the pain I felt at looking at my babies not knowing if I was going to have to leave them and go to prison. Trying to stabilize and not hate the people who helped land me here. I trusted God. I still do today. I hear the threat of the enemy saying I will never be free.

THE REMIX.. CONFUSE THE ENEMY

I will never go back to my old soul contract with him. Even now, awaiting trial, I believe in God alone to get the glory out of this and set me free with no prison time. I'm going to continue to praise him in the hallway until he closes the doors of prison failure and my past and opens the doors of favor that leads to healing, wholeness, new ministry, a new walk, and my new story, filled with his glory. I now realize everything he let me go through was to teach and heal both you and me.

His miracles, he turned my drug-addicted dad into a pastor, he gave my children and me a home and food when I had no job. I'm here alive through it all, still standing to tell you about his glory. This is the death of Jessica Rappit and the birth of Healer Goddess Author Doctor Minister Stephanie Thedford.

CHAPTER 12

MELISSA WILLIAMS

YOUR BEST DAYS ARE AHEAD OF YOUR NOW...

Your best days are ahead of you.

Where you are now is not your end.

The story of your life has a comma, not a period.

The pain you had to live with, you are being healed from TODAY.

You are the head and not the tail.

You are Blessed going in and Blessed going out.

God has not forgotten about you!

YOU are loved by God.

Favor is on your life.

Everything you touch will turn to prophetic Gold.

Your name is clothed with favor.

Doors are swinging open for you.

New Opportunities are chasing you down!

He will restore to you what is needed.

You are healed by the stripes of Jesus; emotionally, mentally, and physically.

There is no good thing He will withhold from you.

You dwell in the secret place of the Highest.

You are loved by the Almighty.

You will LIVE and NOT die but declare the works of the Lord.

No weapon formed against you shall prosper.

You are a Lender & not Borrower.

You are seated in heavenly places.

The Shield of the Lord protects you and those connected to you.

You will walk in the abundance of the Lord.

Your name is associated with greatness

Sickness and disease is far from you.

Your children will arise and call you blessed.

I speak over the life of HER. The guilt, shame, betrayal, heartache, rejection, low self-esteem, loneliness, suicidal thoughts, and any other demonic attachment that has gripped you, bound you, weighed you down and even tried to rob you of your destiny, today by faith, I declare you are healed, delivered and set free!!!

As you and many women like yourself share the stories and testimonies of "HER." These unscripted and life-changing trials to triumph are the life of "a HER." That is a reflection of your new life. She shares your hurt; she's carried your shame. The blessing of her sharing her story is you now have truth and power to embrace. You have "a truth" that the enemy cannot take from you; he will not hold you hostage to your past any longer. The life you have once lived, that in time past made you feel like it was only you that had a hard life; a life no one would dare understand or have lived. But in this chronicle, as you can see, the enemy has no new tricks under the sun. His tactics, strategies, and plots are all the same. To kill, steal and destroy. But your heavenly father has come to reveal to you; you can have a life after this!

Whether You have been ashamed to face it or tell it, or even too hurt to accept it, I wanted the millions of you to have a new glimpse of the hope that God is still able. He's able to heal, restore, rebuild, replenish, and he's able to be all that you need. I know you may still be saying, but how can God do it for me? And I say to you, Why Not? The fact that you have this book is evident it is your time for healing. It's your time to get up and LIVE!!

Join myself and my Co-Authors and the other millions of women around the world as we celebrate YOU!

You were created For This! Everything you need is already inside of you!

As we salute all of the "HERs," we honor You.

THE AUTHORS CORNER

MELISSA F. WILLIAMS

She's a "MOVEMENT"... The Mother, CEO, Minister, Motivational Life Builder, Author, Radio Host & Philanthropist

 **Melissa F. Williams** is a Global Voice for this generation. She is an eclectic trailblazer, who carries a sincere mandate to shift the mindsets of complacency, whether, in spiritual, business, or philanthropic atmospheres, she has been reputed to have a lasting impact on diverse audiences. Melissa Williams is a gifted motivator and business strategist and is a highly requested keynote speaker featured at mass assemblies and conferences, both nationally and abroad. Her nontraditional approach reflects a God-given talent and devotion that she holds with endearment, as she often concludes that "God uses the flawed but Chosen."

Melissa Williams is humbled and honored to submit and serve under the great leadership of Bishop Dreyfus C. Smith, the Pastor, and Founder of Wings of Faith Worldwide MInistries in Atlanta Ga and many other mentors, but not shy of being a significant influence herself, as she has mentored several women nationwide. In 2006, after overcoming several trials in her own life, Melissa launched a multi-dimensional entrepreneurship and community outreach program, servicing women and children both in her local community and nationwide. Melissa Williams Ministry, as well as Daughters of Destiny Inc., were birthed from her heart for servant leadership. Since then, Williams has become a force in her community by successfully spearheading dozens of humanity projects such as offering quality Education, providing Mentorship Programs, Help One Feed One, yearly Toy Drive, Single Parent Childcare assistance, Financial Literacy, GED Prep Courses, and several youth initiative programs. Under the leadership of Melissa Williams, her ministry has provided thousands of school supplies and extensive outreach to many. It is this kind of "hands-on service" that has impacted the lives of her community and provoked her to open Empowerment Centers.

Melissa Williams is the bestselling author of *"Doubt And Destiny Don't Mix," "After This" "10 tips MOVING beyond Heartbreak,"* and her latest title *"The Comeback."* All bodies of work that granted her the opportunity to develop a life coaching clientele with an almost perfect success rate. Pairing what she was commissioned to do spiritually with her enhanced business skill sets, she has been able to influence many female entrepreneurs to walk in professional purpose with excellence.

Melissa Williams has graced dozens of panels, radio shows, podcasts and has been featured in a myriad of magazines.

With all the life-changing things she continues to do, her greatest zeal and reward is being the proud mother of three beautiful children.

KAREN BEVERLY

Karen Beverly is an entrepreneurial single mom who wants to inspire other moms around the world to go after what they want in life. She believes motherhood comes with a wealth of skills that do well in entrepreneurship.

Karen has a background as a human resource representative at a mental health facility. Even though human resource was her career, Karen realized at an early age her passion was rooted in inspiring others. Her inspiration initially came from her angelic voice, as Karen has used her vocal gift to sing around the globe. In her early 30's she realized the traditional workforce would not allow for the time flexibility she desired to pursue her dreams and, more importantly, be a full-time mom for her daughter Jordan, who Karen had while she was still a Senior in High School. At the age of 32, Karen decided to step out on faith to become a full-time work-from-home mom! She is proof that you can reach extraordinary goals, even when the beginning of your journey seems like you are off course.

Karen coaches and leads a team of independent entrepreneurs across the United States and Canada. As a result of her business accomplishments, she was featured in Success From Home magazine in May of 2017. The article focused on Karen as a successful single parent in control of her success working from home. Karen often sings and speaks in arenas filled with thousands of people seeking to become the best version of themselves. Karen has a list of personal accolades; however, she's mostly excited about the number of lives she's been able to directly and indirectly impact. She's a true believer in abundance and has no hesitation in pouring into others.

Karen now resides in Maryland, where she continues to make a living while truly making a difference in people's lives. She attributes her success to great mentors, hard work, perseverance, an incredible team and a firm belief that you should ALWAYS REMEMBER YOU ARE BRAVER THAN YOU BELIEVE, STRONGER THAN YOU SEEM, AND SMARTER THAN YOU THINK.

TIFFANY PEOPLE

Tiffany People was born and raised in Statesboro, Ga. She is the fourth of nine children by her mom and the baby of six by her dad. She's the mother of two handsome boys and two beautiful girls. She's also GiGi to three gorgeous grandsons. Tiffany People is the founder of C.O.R.I Ministry. Her ministry focuses on healing, deliverance, and restoration. She uses her life trials and triumphs as an example for many. She strives to show others how to overcome, survive, live, and heal. Tiffany's passion has always been ministry at a very young age. She received salvation at the age of eleven. At the age of twelve she would experience a loss that would devastate and change her world. The loss of her grandfather who had been raising her since she was two years old. For the next two years she battled depression no one knew about. She said nothing to no one. At the age of fourteen she made her first of many attempts at suicide. But God's love and mercy did grace her. Realizing she was favored by God she began to fight to pursue her dream. By sixteen Tiffany would serve as a nurse to her Pastor who was a Prophet. Her foundation for the prophetic was laid at that time. By eighteen she spoke her first sermon at a youth detention center for girls. Thirty-eight young souls gave their lives to Christ afterward. Tiffany now uses her pain, struggles, trials, and adversity as a platform to help others heal, recover and become more than conquerors. Her force is prayer, the power of God, healing, deliverance and the demonstration of the love of God. Tiffany is very passionate about the lost, the weary and those that seek to give up. Tiffany People wears many hats, but she feels her greatest accomplishment is being a mother. She's also a licensed minister, singer, writer, conference host, speaker, songwriter, role model, and mentor. Her hobbies include music, singing, dancing, and writing.

SHADARIA A. ALLISON

Shadaria A. Allison is the compelling author of several published manuscripts; a motivational speaker, rising advocate for women, and community organizer.

Her freshman release, "Wise as a serpent, Harmless as a Dove": "A Woman's Manual" proved to be a "life-changing" body of work influencing and empowering women of all ages to pursue transparency throughout traumatic life and relationship experiences. Since then, Shadaria has produced thought invoking literature that encourages unity amongst women and the attempt to challenge faith-based organizations and Governmental infrastructures to serve real communal needs. This passion has allowed her to speak at several high schools, churches, and panel discussions. Her altruistic efforts landed state-wide recognition, as she was chosen as an Alabama finalist and presented a medal from **United Ways** *2018 "Ignite Awards"* for community organizers and their innovative approaches towards communal reform; this and many other communal contributions launched her into the forefront of local Birmingham news outlets. Allison was interviewed on both **Fox News and the Birmingham Times** newspaper for her overcoming success story as an impoverished teen mom turned humanitarian.

She has since served on massive community chairs such as the Civil Rights Birmingham *"foot soldiers"* Committee, and **Mayor Woodfin's transitional board for Environmental Justice and sustainability**. Her love and devotion to the historic city of Birmingham sparked the launch of her most recent manuscript series: **Married2theMission: Birmingham A City Destined for reform**.By which she integrates both her passion for literature and her compassion for her beloved city into an all-out <u>campaign</u> to revitalize an abandoned hospital into a state-of-the-art rehab and recreational facility for the impoverished, mentally ill, and drug-addicted individuals.

Her transparency and relatability to the female heart have earned her the endearing nickname as ***"The Woman Whisperer"* and *"Birmingham's Darling."*** She has spoken to hundreds of women ages ranging from teens to the elderly and has been invited to schools and Recreational centers to speak. There is never a dry eye in the place of her absence. A fierce female liberator of her time, Shadaria has been compared to the likes of Coretta Scott King by which she humbly accepts the awe-inspiring connotation.

Though duty calls her many places, her favorite place to be is wherever her son is. Shadaria is the devoted mother of Ca'ren Franklin, who aspires to be an Aerospace engineer and study engineering at Yale University.

Recognized amongst the rising millennial leaders of this generation, Shadaria Allison plans to continue to touch lives. One woman at a time.

TAMIKA LAWRENCE

Tamika Lawrence is a Wife, Mother, and CEO of her own business, "Mechelle Expression Candles." She resides in Odenville, Alabama. She graduated from WEHS in Birmingham, Alabama, and attended LSCC and Herzing Institute. Tamika is passionate about Family, Friendships and serving in Ministry. She attends Revelation Knowledge Bible Church under the leadership of Pastors Larry and Tracy Russell. She serves on the Intercessors Ministry, Music Ministry as a Praise and amp Worship Leader, and Leader of the Girls Mentoring Group. Her husband, Minister Marco, serves as the youth minister, and she works alongside him. They strive to build the next generation by teaching them who they are in Christ and be who God has designed and created them to be. Tamika is currently training under her Pastor to become a licensed minister, and she attends presently Samford University, where she is enrolled in the MIT program.

DEIDRA D. HOLLOWAY

Deidra D. Holloway is the Senior Pastor of Kingdom Choices Ministries in Birmingham Alabama. She's the CEO and Founder of Sources Unlimited Productions, which is a unique media production company serving ministries and companies alike across the nation. Ms.

Holloway developed Kingdom Choices Broadcasting Network currently on Roku and Amazon.

Firestic, where she aires her television show entitled Kairos Live! She created a youth and young adult ministry group, The Jesus Force, that traveled the nation from 2004 through 2007.

Ms. Holloway has faithfully served in the Birmingham Public School system for twenty years

with outstanding integrity under the Department of Finance in Local School Finance. She is a

graduate of Local School Financial Management Certification Program through Alabama School

Business Management. Deidra served in the United States Army and Army Reserves as well as

Army Recruiter for approximately seven years, where she earned several military awards and

rankings. She is a 2007 graduate of Kingdom University!

Deidra Holloway is the daughter of Evelyn and Moses Holloway Jr. She has one brother and

fourteen God-children, which she considers her very own. Her mandate is to make disciples of

Christ out of men and develop a true heart of Sonship! She has a passion for youth and young

adults to manifest victory and deliverance in their everyday lives and to become

OVERCOMERS through Christ Jesus! Her life motto is "To Thine Own Self Be True"!

DR. NIA "JUST NIA" GEE

Dr. Nia puts the Real in Religion. She doesn't preach the traditional religious stories from years past; she makes the Bible relevant to today's time. She teaches forming a relationship with God in your own way. She focuses her ministry to the millennials, underserved and downtrodden, just like Jesus did. While dedicating her life to her ministry she also makes time to educate on multiple platforms: Certified Christian Life Coach, The Just Nia Morning Show, Untold Chronicles Talk Radio on New Praise Radio, Untold Chronicles Magazine, The Destiny Prayer Line, M-brace (women's ministry), School of the Prophets, Dr. Nia: Identity Guru and Onyx News Network Anchor. She wants you to come as you truly are into her judgment-free safe haven. She will arm you with the Word of God to protect you as you move about your day in this unbalanced world we live in. She wholeheartedly believes in Hebrews 13:8-Jesus Christ is the same yesterday and today and forever.

VALERIE SMITH

Valerie began teaching piano/music theory/vocal performance in her senior year of high school and continued her studies as an undergraduate at The University of Alabama at Birmingham with a major in Music. Valerie's first significant role in a musical stage play was her appearance in "Sophisticated Ladies" in 2008. She has recorded with the UAB Gospel Choir on the Sophomore Album, "Lessons for Life," where she led the remake of Deborah Cox's "How Did You Get Here" entitled, " I'm Glad You Got Here." Valerie is also featured on UAB Gospel Choir's 2013 Nu Soul City Album singing lead vocal on the song, "Thank You." Valerie went on to become the Music Director/Minister of Music/Worship. Pastor for a few prominent churches in the city of Birmingham and currently serves as the Minister of Music at Mt. Canaan Full Gospel Church. Valerie is the Founder/President of B Natural Music Group who published her 2011 single "Your Grace," and 2014 single "Break Free." Most notably, Valerie released her EP Album "Dream" (B Natural Music) on December 2, 2016, which debuted on the Gospel Albums Billboard Chart at number 18. Valerie has been featured as an opening artist and shared the stage with Kirk Franklin, Tamala Mann, Jekalyn Carr, Ricky Dillard, Byron Cage, Alexis Spight, J.J. Hairston, and many more! Valerie's highlight moments via the Audiostate team led by the World Renowned Director and Composer, Dr. Henry Panion include vocal directing for the following artists: Robin Thicke, India Arie, LeAnn Rimes, Yolanda Adams, Tony, Toni, Toni and a host of lead vocalist features with Dr. Henry Panion and the Symphony.

JASMINE BROWN

Jasmine Brown A.k.a Sunshine motivational speaker and Business Owner of Sunshine Lash Co. Empowerment Ministry LLC Where she trains students to be the top 10% in the lash industry. By heart Jasmine was born a motivational speaker. She didn't see how the whole picture would come together on how she would use her gift and still obey God on pursuing her purpose. However in 2016 God gave her the vision on how she would merge her lash business and her ministry together to create Sunshine Lash Co. Empowerment. February 18, 2017 Birthed Sunshine Lash Co. Empowerment. First large speaking engagement over 100 people were covered in Maggianos Buckhead Banquet Hall, a room for 80 people. She knew since it was her first event that she should do at least a room for thirty, but God spoke to her heart and said a room for 80. She walked by faith and never looked back. Jasmine is a wife, a mother of 2, the oldest of 4 (3 sisters and one brother.) Jasmine A.K.A Sunshine was once headed to the strip club, being called sunshine as the dancer. Now God is using her as Sunshine for the light that he's using inside of her for his Glory. Jasmine understands Sharing her gift with the world and able to help people find their inner strength is what moves her

"God said he wanted me to go back and save myself. So my goal is to work with young girls from the age of 12 to 19 years old plus many more

APRIL M. VAUGHN

April Vaughn, a quintessential modern-day renaissance woman, has conquered yet another mountain and is emerging as a Kingdom powerhouse with her authorial debut in this epic anthology. The epitome of a God-fearing Proverbs 31 wife, she compliments her husband and works diligently by his side to bring their family's vision to fruition and train up their two beautiful daughters to walk in the ways of the Kingdom. Gaining her collegiate training at the Georgia Institute of Technology, she (the first in her lineage to do so) earned her Bachelor of Science degree in Industrial and Systems Engineering from the #1 program in the country. Through her financial astuteness and aptitude for solving problems, she has since dominated the corporate arena, demolishing the proverbial ladder, crashing through glass ceilings, forging pathways, and bridging organizational gaps for those who are to follow in her footsteps. But she didn't stop there. Her entrepreneurial spirit and fearless nature led her to launch a real estate investment business, staking her claim in territory that was thought to be off-limits. Her mission is to rebuild cities, break the back of poverty, and to create generational wealth for the masses. She has an innately philanthropic heart and a passion for upgrading the lives of those around her. Her life's journey, though not easy, is most certainly not over. With unwavering faith in God, resilience, tenacity, and an industrious fortitude, she has kicked down and walked through doors that no man can close behind her. Those held captives by generational curses, spiritual bondage, and the lies of the enemy will surely be set free by the deliverance of her unbelievably riveting testimony

STEPHANIE THEDFORD

Stephanie Thedford AKA Jessica Rappit is a native of Birmingham, AL, where her humble upbringing set a foundation for her insatiable appetite for a career as an entertainer, entrepreneur, and healer. Jessica Rappit is a rising motivational speaker, entertainer, leader healer of the mind, body and spirit, and style mogul who's known for her thrilling, authentic rap lyrics.

At the tender age of 15, she became a hometown pioneer when starting her entertainment career. Jessica has traveled the United States performing and hosting events, captivating audiences with her Alpha female personality and classic Jessica Rabbit persona. Her public and authentic persona is that of a strong, determined leader that is well-known and respected all over the nation. Her music is a lyrical narrative and satirical commentary on real-life hardships, trials, and tribulations that she overcame while growing up and surviving in a male-dominated city and industry. She speaks on platforms that captivate people by bringing them out of the wilderness with truth. Her hit single "Lyfe" was inspired by her life and journey from the streets to success. Jessica decided to put a pause on her musical career as an indie artist because she felt the Highest was calling her to use her voice to teach and lead instead of polluting the masses with glorification of cars, drugs, and sex

Outside of the studio, Jessica Rappit has experienced the success and the failures of being a business owner but through all she's faced abuse, molestation, divorced, being a single mother, and felon. She still remained humble and kept looking forward; she feels as if her trails are for her to teach from not dwell in. She's a mother of three that has backed her daughters in starting a clothing line called A Summer in London, which will help provide help for single mothers and children with parents that have been murdered through street violence. Jessica's ultimate goal is to reach and inspire those from humble beginnings such as herself to strive for success no matter where they are in life.